Ohio

A Captivating Guide to the History of Ohio and Ulysses S. Grant

Free Bonus from Captivating History (Available for a Limited time)

Hi History Lovers!

Now you have a chance to join our exclusive history list so you can get your first history ebook for free as well as discounts and a potential to get more history books for free! Simply visit the link below to join.

Captivatinghistory.com/ebook

Also, make sure to follow us on Facebook, Twitter and Youtube by searching for Captivating History.

Table of Contents

Part 1: History of Ohio

A Captivating Guide to the People and Events That Shaped the History of the Buckeye State

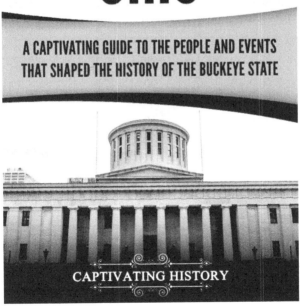

Introduction

The story of the state of Ohio has many different beginnings because Ohio is many different things. There is the land, the rock, the rivers, the hills, and the valleys that trace their beginnings to long before any human set foot there. There were the First People who came to the land many thousands of years ago and formed complicated societies and civilizations. However, one beginning of the state of Ohio, at least as modern humans would recognize it, began as a compromise between two parties that only had a vague notion of what the land and the people who lived there were like.

It was the end of the American Revolutionary War. As the two sides, the Americans and the British, were settling their dispute in Paris, the Americans declared their former masters needed to give up not just the Thirteen Colonies but also the land that would be called the Northwest Territory north of the Ohio River. The British did not like this request, but the Americans made it clear they were willing to take back up their arms over this point. So, the British acquiesced.

This land, which few in the colonies had seen, was suddenly a part of the new nation. This new possession would eventually become five separate states: Ohio, Indiana, Illinois, Michigan, and Wisconsin. Most people of the time simply called the area Ohio, and the rush to settle this new land was called "Ohio Fever."

Many reports made their way into newspapers in the east, especially in New England, of a land of fabulous opportunity. The soil was healthy, the game abundant, and the rivers clear and fast flowing. The first group of American settlers was led by Brigadier General Rufus Putnam, who was famous for his fortifications of the Dorchester Heights that surprised the British at Boston. He helped to form the Ohio Company of Associates, which set about to purchase and settle the Northwest Territory. Putnam brought along a group of soldiers, scouts, blacksmiths, farmers, and adventurers who saw a chance for greatness in Ohio. They built and boarded ships that sent them down the Ohio River. Eventually, they came to a spot where the Muskingum and Ohio Rivers met and formed a settlement. It would be known as Marietta, and it would be the first American town in what would become the state of Ohio.

Chapter 1 – The Northwest Ordinance

Putnam and his followers were not the first Americans to settle in the area. Various waves of squatters had moved across the Allegheny Mountains and the Ohio River to make a life in what they saw as an untamed wilderness. These squatters created impromptu settlements, but they did not last and were not officially recognized. Before these people, there had been British and French fur traders who crossed through the forests and paddled along the streams, but even they were not the first humans to see this land and enjoy its bounty.

The first settlers of what would one day be Ohio were the Native Americans, such as the Shawnee, Lenape, and Wyandot. They hunted whitetail deer, black bears, beavers, otters, turkeys, ducks, geese, squirrels, and mountain lions. The skies were sometimes filled with huge flocks of passenger pigeons and Carolina parakeets. The Native Americans traded with the Europeans, handing over deer, bear, and beaver skins and furs for clothes, metal pots, and tools. The Native Americans also grew corn, beans, and squash in meadows and fields. The name Ohio is derived from the Iroquois word, *O-y-o*, which means "great river."

In 1787, the Confederation Congress, the ruling body of the United States of America from 1781 to 1789, passed An Ordinance for the Government of the Territory of the United States North-

West of the River Ohio. However, since that name is a mouthful, almost everyone called it the Northwest Ordinance. The Northwest Ordinance established the means by which the government could sell this land to settlers and the method by which this territory could be turned into new states. The ordinance went through various revisions but finally allowed a large portion of land to be purchased by Putnam's Ohio Company. It also established something unique: slavery would be prohibited in the entire region.

The Ohio Company's plan required the establishment of public schools and universities. The land was also partially given to Revolutionary War veterans in lieu of unpaid wages. This relieved the new government of a large debt and put millions of dollars into its coffers, which helped to keep the country financially stable. The men who were led by General Putnam were almost all veterans, and when they landed at the confluence of the Ohio and Muskingum, they discovered they would have neighbors.

This was not a surprise; it was well understood the lands were already inhabited by Native Americans. The settlers of the Ohio Company were directed to engage in peace agreements with the native whenever possible. The general opinion was that there was enough land for everyone. These new arrivals were apparently not a surprise to the Native Americans either.

Putnam found a group of Lenape (or Delaware) warriors camped near their new settlement. The members of the Wolf Clan were led by Chief Hopocan, known in the historical record as Captain Pipe. But before we dive into their interaction, a bit of background is needed on the Lenape. After the French and Indian War (1754-1763), the Lenape moved out of Pennsylvania into the Ohio Country. They had moved because of white settlers encroaching on their lands. The British promised the Ohio region would be free of white settlers. This, of course, did not hold true. Pipe tried to remain neutral during the Revolutionary War, but after the Lenape were attacked by American forces that eventually destroyed a Lenape village, Pipe allied with the British. In 1782, Pipe defeated forces led by Colonel William Crawford. In retaliation for an event known as the Moravian massacre, where ninety-six pacifist Christian Native Americans had been executed by American soldiers, Pipe captured, tortured, and killed Colonel

Crawford. It was said Pipe had painted Crawford's face black, marking him for a most gruesome death. And it was gruesome; he was tortured for hours before being burned at the stake.

Putnam knew all of this when he met Pipe, but the two agreed to live peacefully together. However, Putnam remained suspicious of the Native Americans who lived in the Ohio Country.

Besides the Lenape, Ohio was home to the Wyandot, Shawnee, and Cherokee, to name a few. The Native Americans' concept of land ownership was distinctive to each tribe and each group within that tribe. It was common for one tribe to lend another tribe hunting grounds for a season or more. In fact, many of the Native American groups that lived in Ohio when Putnam's settlement began were new arrivals themselves, having recently left their ancestral lands due to the encroachment of white settlers. Still, the Native Americans were learning that promises from the government were hardly worth the paper on which they were printed. The settlers, for their part, always eyed the Native Americans with caution. Putnam himself felt the Lenape and Wyandots seemed peaceful, but he did not care for the Mingos, Shawnee, or Cherokee.

At Putnam's settlement, the future Marietta, new people arrived every week. Massive trees needed to be felled and land cleared for houses, farmland, and other buildings. The wood was plentiful, and the soil was just as rich as had been reported. Putnam planned to build a large blockade around the town, complete with watchtowers. The settlers discovered ancient earthworks nearby, large mounds with what appeared to be ramps and walkways. The names of the people who built these mounds, which can be found throughout Ohio, have been lost, but modern archaeologists call them the Hopewell Culture. The settlers were very impressed with these works and felt they were equal to any ancient ruins in Europe or Asia. They had no way of knowing the mounds were around one thousand years old.

It is easy to think of the settlers as nameless faces working to build a home. So, let's introduce a few of the more notable inhabitants. Dr. Jabez True was the first physician to arrive in Ohio. Paul Fearing was the first attorney. And Mary Owen, a nurse, was the first woman to join the settlement.

Putnam and the Ohio Company were not the only Americans who had moved to the Northwest Territory. General Arthur St. Clair was appointed governor of the region in 1787. John Cleves Symmes, a judge from New Jersey and supporter of the Revolution, bought a tract of land in what is now southwest Ohio amounting to 311,682 acres for roughly $225,000 in 1788. A small settlement, consisting of two houses and a few log cabins named Losantiville, was built on the Ohio River.

Part of the agreement between the government and Symmes was that fifteen acres would be set aside for the federal government for the construction of a fort. In the summer of 1789, Fort Washington was built close to Losantiville. It was an impressive structure meant to house 1,500 soldiers and protect any nearby settlers from Native American aggression. St. Clair renamed the town of Losantiville to Cincinnati after the Society of Cincinnati, of which he was president, which, in turn, gets its name from the legendary Roman Cincinnatus.

By the time of Fort Washington's construction, Native Americans and whites were in an undeclared war in Ohio. The soldiers there were under the command of General Josiah Harmar. In 1790, Harmar began a campaign to defeat the Miami and Shawnee, who were raiding settlements in Ohio. He had 1,453 troops, including regular soldiers and many militiamen, some of whom he considered utterly worthless, under his command. They headed for the main Miami village in what is today Fort Wayne, Indiana.

Harmar, Putnam, and St. Clair were in a difficult position. President George Washington and Congress expected them to maintain peace in the Ohio Country and encouraged settlements but understood it would mean conflict with Native Americans and a need for more troops. Despite this need for men, Congress lowered the salaries of enlisted men to only two dollars a month, while officers received anywhere between eighteen to sixty dollars a month. This made recruiting exceptionally hard. Leaders like Harmar were faced with trying to subdue the Native Americans by force without enough manpower.

Not wanting to alarm the British to the north or the peaceful Native Americans in the Northwest Territory, Secretary of War

Henry Knox sent runners ahead of Harmar's forces to let these groups know they were not targets. But because of this, the true targets, the Miami and Shawnee, knew Harmar was headed their way before he had even left Fort Washington. The Shawnee were led by Blue Jacket, while Little Turtle commanded the Miami tribe. These two war chiefs knew they needed to defend their land at all costs. They realized the Americans had greater firepower, but they also knew they would be slow in making their way through an unknown land. So, they took every advantage they could get.

When Harmar arrived at the Miami village, he found it burned and empty. He hoped this meant the Native Americans had fled west for good, but he was also concerned he had lost them. Harmar's force found another abandoned village, and his men began looting. However, Little Turtle had a force in the woods beyond this village. His men opened fire on the distracted Americans, who quickly panicked.

Harmar began a retreat but was surprised by Native Americans at every turn. By the time his forces returned to Fort Washington, their supplies were gone, and the militiamen were close to mutiny. The campaign had been a complete disaster. While a court determined that Harmar had done the best he could, his career was finished, and he was replaced by Governor St. Clair, who took up the command in March 1791.

However, St. Clair faced the same hardships as his predecessor. Secretary of War Knox had promised close to three thousand regulars. Instead, the governor had only 2,300 men, most of whom were not regulars but ill-trained militia. The low wages for militiamen (some records state it was as low as one dollar a month) meant the men who signed up were not those who had much self-discipline or a desire to fight.

By this time, Cincinnati had many more settlers and businesses, including brothels and taverns. St. Clair moved his men out of Fort Washington primarily to get away from such establishments. He was already five weeks behind schedule.

St. Clair established Fort Hamilton, which would eventually become the city of Hamilton, in 1791. The fort was built well but delayed the expedition further, causing St. Clair's forces to continue their march into the inhospitable weather. An incompetent pack master caused them to lose horses at an alarming rate. The provisions were not enough, and morale suffered.

The forces separated themselves into four groups: officers, regulars, levies, and militiamen. The militiamen were determined to be loathsome and untrustworthy. The levies (who had been recruited for a shorter period than regulars) were not much better than the militia. The regulars were considered rude, and the officers distrusted one another. St. Clair was unable to blend the groups together, which proved to be a source of many problems. On top of this, the change in weather brought sickness and fatigue. Two men were executed for desertion.

All the while, Blue Jacket's and Little Turtle's scouts kept them informed of the enemy's position and strength. They knew that St. Clair was floundering. They also knew that on October 31ª, sixty militiamen had deserted St. Clair, who sent a large party after them. They knew the enemy was no longer putting up fortifications around their encampments and that there were few guards posted at night. The Native Americans were in high spirits as they made their way toward the American contingent. Among them was a young scout who had proved particularly helpful to the war chiefs. His name was Tecumseh.

The Native Americans, only three hundred in number, attacked at dawn on November 4th, 1791. The warriors were from many different tribes and people. The Wyandots and Iroquois attacked St. Clair's right side, while the Shawnee, Miami, and Lenape attacked the center. St. Clair's left was hit by the Ottawa, Ojibwa, and Potawatomi tribes. The warriors came from these nations, but that does not mean everyone in that nation was at war with white settlers. Villages, clans, and individuals acted independently.

Even though the Native Americans were outnumbered, the surprise attack was extremely successful. After three hours of fighting, the Native Americans completely routed the American forces, many of whom turned and fled as soon as the opportunity arose. St. Clair had two horses shot out from under him but managed to get on a third and eventually left with his men. The wounded and dead were left behind in a blind panic. Of the two hundred women who followed the army, only three escaped. St. Clair lost an unknown number to desertion during the battle. Once the survivors made it back to Fort Washington, many more deserted. St. Clair had perhaps finally pushed them too far when he ordered them to pay for any lost rifles or horses.

The Native Americans had been especially careful to target officers, who displayed insignia and commanded from horseback, which made them excellent targets. Of the 124 officers with St. Clair, 69 were killed or seriously wounded. The Native Americans reported only twenty-one deaths. Knowing the fate of General Harmar, St. Clair carefully considered how to present his report to Secretary of War Henry Knox.

The total casualties for St. Clair's soldiers were 623 killed and 258 wounded. It was the deadliest battle American forces had seen up to that date, deadlier than any battle in the Revolution. There was nothing St. Clair could do but report those numbers. When President Washington received the news, he was enraged. He demanded St. Clair's resignation, which he received in March 1792. St. Clair remained the governor of the Northwest Territory. The battle he fought against Little Turtle and Blue Jacket has come to be known as "St. Clair's Defeat." He was eventually removed from office by President Thomas Jefferson.

Meanwhile, all of this activity cast a shadow on General Putnam and the Ohio Company's settlement, now called Marietta after Marie Antoinette, who had much to help the American cause. The town was continuing to grow, but the people were receiving news from all around that the Native Americans were intent on pushing the Americans out of the Ohio Country. It was said that one Native American had said that within the year, there would be no smoke coming from any cabins along the Ohio River.

Leaders emerged from the town's founders, most notably Colonel Ebenezer Sproat, who became a commander of the militia. Sproat was over six feet tall, and the friendly Native Americans named him "Hetuck," meaning "eye of the buck." He would be remembered as "Big Buckeye" and might be the source of Ohio's nickname: the Buckeye State.

For their part, Little Turtle and Blue Jacket pursued an alliance with the British in the hopes of stopping the Americans' encroachment. Both of the chiefs knew that while their defeat of St. Clair had been thorough, the Americans would surely return.

Chapter 2 – Fallen Timbers

The American army did not return to the battlefield against the Native Americans for two years after St. Clair's Defeat. In the meantime, the Native Americans continued to raid and harass settlements and forts throughout Ohio. Soldiers were stationed at these forts but not in large numbers. They were not prepared to attack the Native Americans in return. The settlers did the best they could to defend their plots and families. The Native Americans failed to undermine the Americans' conviction to stay in Ohio.

At the same time, the federal government worked on increasing the military budget to bring the army up to five thousand men. The plan was for these men to go to the Northwest Territory and rid the entire region of the Native American threat. They chose General Anthony Wayne, another member of the Society of Cincinnati and hero from the American Revolution, as the new commander. He had been given the nickname "Mad Anthony" due to his fiery temperament as a commander.

Wayne's legacy before his command cannot be viewed favorably through the lens of retrospection. After the Revolutionary War, he mortgaged his family's estate in Pennsylvania to buy a plantation and several slaves in Georgia. He came to believe that America should be governed by an aristocratic elite class and that the government should be used as a tool to promote their interests. When he won a congressional seat, an investigation revealed that his campaign manager had engaged in clear election fraud. Wayne was eventually removed from office. When he was selected to lead the army against the Native Americans in the Ohio Country, his wife had already left him, he was bankrupt, and he had no clear prospects. Thus, he eagerly jumped at this new opportunity, though he knew the job would be a hard one.

Wayne began to recruit new soldiers in the spring of 1792. Learning from the mistakes of previous generals, he established an area to house the soldiers away from the temptations of the settlements. He also created a camp called Legionville, where new recruits could be systematically trained and drilled for combat with the Native Americans. Wayne knew the Native Americans were being assisted by the British, who hoped to dismantle America's hopes for expansion. He also knew the Native Americans felt they were justified in their aggression, as they were trying to retain their land. The general thus came to the conclusion that there would be no peace or a chance for America to advance unless the Native Americans were removed from the area and respected the authority of the United States government. He felt this was his mission in Ohio.

By April 1793, Wayne felt he had enough well-trained soldiers to battle the Native Americans over possession of the land northwest of the Ohio River. In Cincinnati and the nearby settlement of Columbia, settlers issued rewards for Native American scalps. A subscription system was implemented in which anyone who paid into the general fund would receive $130 for the first ten scalps, while non-subscribers only got $100 per scalp.

The Native Americans continually attacked supply wagons and boats that were bringing supplies down the Ohio River. The arrival of Wayne's five-thousand-man army at Fort Washington instilled hope in the settlers. Wayne continued to drill and train his men in mock battles, trying to encourage them to think and fight, not panic and run. A delegation of leaders tried to establish some form of peace with the British and the Native Americans, but they told Wayne no peace could be met because they could not agree upon their demands.

The Lenape, Miami, and Shawnee felt the border needed to be the Ohio River and that all the settlers who had crossed that divide needed to be sent back. The British hoped that a Native American reserve might be established and that the southern border should also be the Ohio River, but they ignored the Americans' arguments that their control of the land had been given up in the Treaty of Paris. The Iroquois Confederacy could come to no agreement because their lands had already been lost east of the Muskingum River. The Americans indicated they were willing to pull back but not all the way to the Ohio River. War seemed inevitable.

Despite the desertion of almost five hundred volunteers from Kentucky, Wayne advanced north and west from Fort Washington. He founded a new fort, Fort Greenville, where he planned to spend the winter. However, Wayne changed his mind and decided to pick up the march in December. He built a fort at the site of St. Clair's infamous defeat. They arrived at the spot on Christmas Day 1793 and began construction of Fort Recovery. The bones of St. Clair's soldier still littered the ground, and Wayne's men buried them in the hard winter soil.

The British became aware of Wayne's movements and helped to organize and advise the various Native American tribes on how to defend their land. The British built Fort Miami in what is today northern Ohio to curb Wayne's advance north. The Native Americans took this to mean the British would support and aid them in their fight against the Americans, but this belief would prove misplaced.

By 1794, America had become Britain's largest trading partner. Added to this was the fact that Britain was a global superpower with interests around the world. They were not interested in a war with America at that time, so Fort Miami would be more of a gesture than a promise.

The Native Americans sent an emissary to Wayne with an overture of peace, but Wayne demanded that every chief had to come to him. He also insisted that they release all white prisoners. Little Turtle and Blue Jacket were not interested. Wayne prepared for war, including the possibility of battling the British. He had been given the authority, directly from President Washington, to take any appropriate actions, including firing on British soldiers if need be.

In June 1794, the Native Americans made the first move and attacked a 360-horse pack train two hundred yards from Fort Recovery. The attack was successful. Emboldened by their victory, the Native Americans planned a night attack on the fort itself. However, the riflemen stationed at the fort put their many hours of training to the test, and the battle went into the morning. The Native Americans finally retreated when it became obvious this plan was futile.

Little Turtle, who had defeated both Harmar and St. Clair, now saw clearly that the Native Americans needed full British support to defeat the Americans. He traveled to Detroit (modern-day Michigan), which was then still in possession of the British, and requested men and cannons. They gave him nothing. Little Turtle was convinced that without this assistance, the Native Americans could not win against Wayne's large, well-trained army.

Wayne set out with his legion, finding abandoned Native American villages along the way. By August, they had reached the rapids of the Maumee River that flows into Lake Erie. They built Fort Deposit and planned to continue toward the British Fort Miami.

The Native Americans under the command of Blue Jacket were determined to stop Wayne in a wooded area known as the Wilderness. Wayne's men reached the spot on August 20th, and fighting erupted. However, unlike earlier battles, the American soldiers retreated but were able to reform their battle lines. There was no panic and disorder; Wayne's endless drilling had done its work. The skirmish only lasted an hour but would be remembered forever afterward as the Battle of the Fallen Timbers.

This time, the Native Americans ran from the battlefield. Those who hoped to find safety at Fort Miami instead found the doors barred against their entry.

Wayne and his men delighted in their victory. Yet, what really drove the Native Americans to reconsider their position was not so much the battle as the truth that the British were not going to help them in any substantial way. The only whites who fought on the side of the Native Americans was a small Canadian regiment of militiamen who had no real authority with the British command.

Wayne did not attack Fort Miami, and the British did not fire on the Americans, so war was avoided for the time being.

The Native Americans came to understand Chief Little Turtle's argument. While they had fought and died against the Americans, the British had remained mere spectators. In November 1794, the Wyandots told Wayne they were ready to bury the hatchet deep in the ground. Blue Jacket arrived at Fort Greenville in February 1795 and accepted Wayne's terms. The Ojibwa, Ottawa, Potawatomi, Miami, and Lenape all came to agreements with Wayne.

The Treaty of Greenville was finally settled in August 1795. It gave almost all of the land that would become the state of Ohio to the Americans, while the Native Americans agreed to leave and settle to the west in what Wayne called Indian Territory. It would eventually be christened Indiana. White settlers could now spread into the Great Miami Valley without fear of conflict with Native Americans.

Little Turtle accepted the terms of the treaty and came to believe that peaceful coexistence between Native Americans and whites was the best solution. Along with the rest of the Native Americans who signed the treaty, he moved west, leaving Ohio to the Americans.

While the Native Americans viewed the boundaries established by the Treaty of Greenville as permanent, the white settlers saw them more as temporary until they needed more land to expand. "Ohio Fever" was still a reality, and now that the threat of Native American attacks seemed somewhat nullified, more settlers were encouraged to make the journey. They purchased acreage from speculators like Judge Symmes, who sometimes sold land they did not technically own. Also, perhaps due to simple error, Symmes sometimes sold plots of land to more than one person without realizing it. He also sold land on credit but failed to pursue payment. This caused the federal government to rethink its qualifications for the sale of territory. It decided to no longer deal with private interests but only with land companies and small-scale speculators.

Still, thanks to the Land Act of 1796, which raised the minimum price of Ohio land from $1 per acre to $2, the land Symmes and others had bought from the government was now worth twice as much. Ohio was proving to be profitable, which only increased its fevered settlement.

By 1796, most of Ohio had been bought by speculators. The most appealing lands were those of the Symmes Purchase, the land of the Ohio Company, the Virginia District, the US Military District, and areas eventually known as the Connecticut Western Reserve and Congress Lands.

These areas would eventually include the major cities of Cleveland, Dayton, Cincinnati, and its eventual capital Columbus. Settlers did not always have the cash to pay for the land, so they might pay partly with corn, livestock, and whiskey. They could also essentially rent land for a few years and then move on, in the process clearing the land and improving it, thus making it worth more for the owner, who could then sell it at a premium price.

Many of those who surveyed Ohio land were paid in acreage, which they could turn around and sell or operate as a home or business. Land was often offered for commercial farming, and land that had rivers or streams was particularly valued because it could be improved with a mill. Like other "fevers," people were motivated in large part by the prospect of financial reward. However, this was not like finding gold or silver deposits. Ohio's value lay in the productivity of the land itself, which could be used for crops, livestock, mills, docks, and so on. Speculators sometimes hired laborers to clear the land, increasing its value, and then sold it for a large profit.

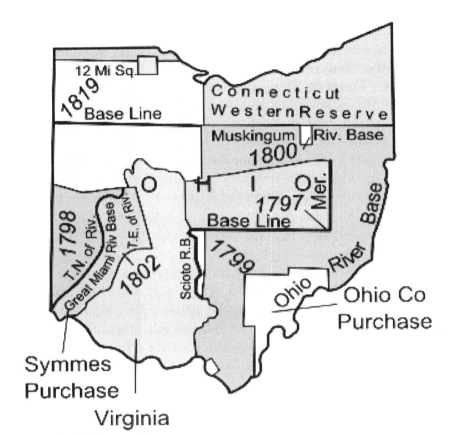

The Ohio Country was subdivided into purchases and government lands.
https://commons.wikimedia.org/wiki/File:Ohio_Lands.svg

By the end of the 18th century, the United States was changing, and the Northwest Territory saw many changes as well. In December 1799, George Washington died of a contracted illness. At the time, John Adams was president, but that wouldn't last for long. Thomas Jefferson beat John Adams in the 1800 presidential election, putting Democratic-Republicans in control instead of the Federalists. The same political climate could be found in the Ohio Country as well. In 1800, the capital of the Northwest Territory was established: Chillicothe. There, several delegates met to create a constitution. Of all the debates and considerations, perhaps the most remarkable was that they agreed to continue the prohibition of slavery. It would be a land consisting of free men and women.

Also, in 1800, a new industry began along the banks of the Ohio River: shipbuilding. Large river boats, able to carry several tons of cargo, were constructed of the abundant timber found in the Northwest Territory. These ships were sent sailing down the Ohio into the Mississippi River and eventually to New Orleans, where they could sell their cargo. Some of the boats went even farther, sailing into the Gulf of Mexico. The route they established from the Ohio Country to the Mississippi River would become an important shipping corridor for the new nation. Ohio's natural resources were already important to the country's future.

At the beginning of the 19th century, Congress enacted legislation that allowed settlers to buy land on credit and also pay off their debt in yearly installments. This meant that settlers of lesser means could buy small tracts of land directly from the government and avoid the issues previous buyers had faced. These settlers cleared land and created small farms throughout the region. They formed towns, which began to dot the landscape in larger and larger numbers. In a short amount of time, the population of the Ohio Country had grown tremendously. Not only that but roads were also being built to connect the various settlements. For instance, a road was forged from the growing town of Marietta to the capital of Chillicothe.

Despite the congressional acts, people still preferred buying land from land speculators, despite the potential pitfalls. This was mainly due to the fact that cash was in short supply. The government required payment in legal tender, but speculators continued to accept goods, including rye and iron nails. The territory's economy was still largely based on a bartering system, but there were some settlers who were conspicuously wealthy. They were sparse in number, but large brick houses began to appear, and people even planned out formal English gardens. On an island in the Ohio River, Mr. and Mrs. Blennerhassett built a large opulent estate and befriended many settlers in Ohio. Because their island was technically part of Virginia (what would become Kentucky), they were able to own a large number of slaves.

Chapter 3 – Statehood

In the spring of 1796, General Moses Cleaveland led a party into the northern wilderness of Ohio. They founded a settlement on the shores of Lake Erie called Cleveland. Accounts differ on why the first "a" was dropped from the name, but it stuck. General Cleaveland left before the end of the year and never returned. The Connecticut Land Company purchased the part of Ohio where Cleveland was.

By 1800, one report said that only three men lived in Cleveland and that two of them were going to leave by the end of the year. The issue was likely the high price of land. It was twice as much as what settlers were willing to pay. Consequently, Cleveland struggled to gain prominence at the beginning of the 19th century, but its location, where the Cuyahoga River flowed into Lake Erie, would prove to be an opportunity that could only wait so long.

Other towns fared much better in the early 1800s. The town of Hudson, located southeast of Cleveland and founded by David Hudson, gained prosperity quickly, partially thanks to the land being sold for $1 to $2 per acre, which was much more in line with what settlers expected. In 1790, Nathaniel Massie founded Massie's Station, which would become Manchester in the Virginia Military District. Naming towns "stations" became very popular. Israel Ludlow, a founder of Cincinnati, established his own settlement named Ludlow's Station. However, the site was abandoned due to fear of Native American attacks. Ludlow went on to plot out the cities of Dayton and Hamilton, which prospered.

Notably, there was also Gallipolis, which had been founded by five hundred French settlers escaping the violence of the French Revolution. They purchased it from the Scioto Company. The only problem was that the Scioto Company did not actually own the land the town was on. The land was actually owned by the Ohio Company. The federal government awarded the people land in Scioto County, but some remained in Gallipolis and thus had to pay for their land twice. Though the French settlers were unaccustomed to such work, they cleared land and built defenses. Their descendants prospered thanks to their hard work. Mount Pleasant was founded as part of another land speculation but came to be the home of a large number of Quakers, who built their first meeting house west of the Alleghenies in the town.

While these towns were important centers, it is just as important to note that many people were living and working on farms. They raised hogs, and the pork industry grew rapidly, especially on the Ohio River at Cincinnati, which was nicknamed "Porkopolis." Farmers grew corn, but it was more economical to feed it to hogs or turn it into whiskey than to ship it directly to market. Due to the flow of the water and the limitation of technology, goods often went from Ohio to New Orleans and from there to the eastern part of the country. Pork was especially prized because the pigs could be brought to slaughterhouses in cities. There, the meat could be dried and salted and then make its way to the Atlantic without spoiling. Beef wasn't so easily processed, but there were still cattle farms in Ohio, along with dairy farms that would mainly produce cheese.

One of the most popular crops at the time was apples. In Ohio Company land, settlers were often required to plant about fifty apple trees on their properties. In 1800, a settler from Pennsylvania arrived with apple seeds acquired from cider mills. His name was John Chapman. Chapman, also known as Johnny Appleseed, was an eccentric but driven man who traveled the Ohio Country planting apple trees and giving away seeds and live plants. He is often described as traveling barefoot and wearing shabby clothing, even in winter. Later depictions of him show him wearing a pot for a hat. These depictions are likely exaggerations, though. He was generally welcomed wherever he went, even by Native Americans.

While everyone else in the Ohio Country was cutting down trees, Chapman was busy planting them.

When Thomas Jefferson entered the White House in 1801, he began a process of extreme land expansion for the country. He believed, as did many whites at the time, that Native Americans would give up land to white settlers who needed it. He was also convinced that Native Americans simply needed to be educated in the agricultural practices of the white Americans. Once they were taught these practices, they would adopt them and forgo their previous methods of living. If Native Americans didn't go along with his designs, Jefferson relied on force and cunning to get their lands regardless.

William Henry Harrison, who at the time was the governor of the Indiana Territory, formed treaties with Native Americans. These treaties saw the Native Americans selling much of the land that would become the states of Indiana and Illinois. The Native Americans grew resentful of their treatment and angry that the Treaty of Greenville had become completely worthless.

Jefferson wanted Ohio to become a state. It was controlled largely by his fellow Democratic-Republicans, who argued for a small central government. Jefferson was able to remove Arthur St. Clair, a Federalist, as governor of the Northwest Territory after St. Clair gave a rebellious speech at the Ohio Constitutional Convention. The Federalists made the point that Ohio did not, in fact, have the required population of sixty thousand to become a state. This was true, but Congress felt otherwise and passed an act enabling Ohio to become a state anyway.

The Constitutional Convention met on November 1ˢᵗ, 1802, to talk about Ohio's possible statehood. Thirty-five delegates attended the convention, twenty-six of whom were Democratic-Republicans. As a result, Ohio's statehood was accepted. The Constitution had a strong anti-government and anti-tax framework; the governor had no veto powers, for instance. The right to vote was given only to white men who paid taxes. African Americans were disenfranchised by a small majority.

On February 19ᵗʰ, 1803, Ohio became the seventeenth state of the United States of America. However, the date is celebrated on March 1ˢᵗ because this was when the Ohio State Legislature met for the first time. Edward Tiffin, an English-born Virginian who came to Chillicothe to practice medicine, became the first governor. His brother-in-law, Thomas Worthington, became one of Ohio's first senators. Tiffin and Worthington, both Democratic-Republicans, were leaders of what was called the Chillicothe Junto, which controlled politics in Ohio for many years.

With official statehood came many improvements. One such institution, which had been in the works for many years, was the creation of the American Western University, later named Ohio University, in the town of Athens. This university, the first of its kind in the new state, was the vision of the Ohio Company's founding members: Manasseh Cutler and Rufus Putnam. While the university was officially founded in 1804, it would not open its doors until 1808 and only had one professor and three students.

Meanwhile, the Native Americans who were still in Ohio and nearby areas were suffering from hunger and poverty, especially the Shawnee, Lenape, and Wyandots. These groups were supposed to have had the northern part of the state to themselves, at least according to the treaties they had signed, but white settlers continued to squat on their land. Some Native Americans tried to learn the way of the white man, as Jefferson had hoped, but many refused to give up their traditional way of life. Jefferson's approach to these people was to hope that the government could force so much debt upon them that the Native Americans would have no option but to sell their lands to settle their debt.

However, a new development captured Jefferson's and the rest of the nation's attention. In 1804, Aaron Burr, the vice president of the US, shot and killed former Secretary of the Treasury Alexander Hamilton. The loss of Hamilton signaled the beginning of the end for the Federalists, but it was also the end of Burr's future in politics. Burr was vilified in the press, but he did not feel inclined to admit defeat. He began toying with the notion of separating the western states from the eastern ones, as well as obtaining land in Louisiana or perhaps Mexico and setting up a new nation with him as the head. He eventually persuaded Mr. and Mrs. Blennerhassett, who lived on the island in the Ohio River near the town of Marietta, to fund his conspiracy to create a new nation in North America.

The year before Burr killed Hamilton, Jefferson had completed the Louisiana Purchase, buying most of the land west of the Mississippi River all the way into the current states of Montana, Wyoming, and Colorado. It did not stretch all the way to the Pacific Coast, as is often imagined. This gave the United States the prosperous port of New Orleans. By 1806, this jewel was in Burr's and Blennerhassett's sights. The exact plan remains unclear, but it involved Blennerhassett funding the recruiting of thousands of soldiers and the construction of a large fleet to transport them down the Ohio River. Burr also conspired with General James Wilkinson, the governor of the Louisiana Territory. Burr also courted the British and had supporters among elites in New Orleans.

The plan began to unravel when Blennerhassett started turning his island into a military outpost. Burr traveled the western states, and rumors of his plans began to trickle back to Washington, DC. Finally, Wilkinson, who now believed Burr's plan would fail, sent a letter directly to Jefferson, outlining Burr's plan without naming the former vice president directly. However, Jefferson already knew that Burr was planning something. Ohio militia overtook Blennerhassett Island and ransacked it but found it mostly empty. When Burr and Blennerhassett met up on the Ohio, instead of the thousand or more soldiers Burr had requested, Blennerhassett could only provide about one hundred. They still continued with their plan, but their southern support faded.

Burr, who was now a wanted man, was captured in Bayou Pierre, Louisiana, in 1807 and sent to Richmond, Virginia, to stand trial. Despite the evidence of a plan, Burr and Blennerhassett were acquitted because Justice John Marshall did not feel their actions matched the definition of treason described in the Constitution. However, the public viewed Burr with complete contempt. He was burned in effigy across the nation. He fled to England for a while, where he attempted to convince Britain and France to invade America but failed. Eventually, he returned to New York City, where he worked as a lawyer, his imperial dreams now gone.

The people of Ohio particularly despised Burr because his scheme counted on the state seceding from the rest of the country, something that most people did not support. Part of this was due to the fact that they were, for the most part, from the eastern states and had only recently arrived. In fact, the number of people pouring into Ohio is something to marvel at. From 1800 to 1820, the total population went from 45,365 to 230,760. It was an unprecedented rate of growth.

In 1807, Governor Tiffin resigned from his position to become the US senator of Ohio. This meant that the speaker of the Ohio Senate, Thomas Kirker, became the new governor. Kirker had been born in Ireland; he immigrated to the US when he was nineteen. By 1792, he was living in Manchester in Adams County. Kirker should have only served less than a year, but at the next gubernatorial election, it was determined that the winner, Return Meigs Jr., was not eligible because he had not lived in the state for the required four years before running.

Kirker was replaced at the next election by Samuel Huntington, another Democratic-Republican and resident of the small town of Cleveland. The major issue during Huntington's term was the judicial review, or the Supreme Court's authority on the review of the validity of a legislative act. Huntington supported judicial review, and his side eventually won this dispute.

Jonathan Meigs Jr., who had been disqualified from being governor in 1808, entered the picture again. Huntington did not pursue a second term in 1810, and Meigs became governor, serving until 1814. Meigs had been a practicing lawyer in Marietta, then became postmaster, and then became a territorial court judge in 1798. He served in various capacities in the public sector and eventually sat on the Supreme Court of Ohio. He then went to a posting in Louisiana and even served as a judge in Michigan Territory. It was at this time that he decided to run for governor, but he had lived too long out of state to qualify, despite winning the election.

During Meigs's tenure, it was finally determined that the state capital should not be in Chillicothe or Zanesville but in a central location. The capital of Columbus was founded in 1812, and construction began on a state house and state penitentiary.

While all of the official work of statehood was undertaken, the fear of Native American attacks and the chance for war continued to be an issue. In 1805, a Native American named Lalawethika suffered from a seizure that left him unconscious for an extended period of time. Lalawethika was the younger brother of the Shawnee Chief Tecumseh, and before his coma, he had been considered a particularly worthless alcoholic of little importance. His family was certain he would die, but instead, he returned to the waking world with a message. He told those around him that he had gone to the spirit world and been shown that the Native Americans who had abandoned their traditional ways of life and succumbed to drink and excess were destined to live in something like hell for all eternity.

Tecumseh was a Shawnee war chief who fought to push the Americans out of Ohio.
https://commons.wikimedia.org/wiki/File:Tecumseh02.jpg

Lalawethika told anyone that would listen that whites were children of the Evil Spirit and allies of the Great Serpent. They could not be trusted and should be considered the enemies of the Shawnee and other tribes. He said the tribes must all come together and push the whites out of their land and reclaim what they had given up. He also told them that he was no longer Lalawethika but Tenskwatawa or the "Prophet."

He preached his message, and many of the young Native Americans, especially men, were stirred by his words. Tenskwatawa began to gather supporters in a village near Greenville, and reports were soon being spread that the group, which included the Lenape and Wyandots, were painting and putting feathers on their tomahawks, clear signs of war.

Tecumseh joined his brother, but a shortage of food in Greenville meant they needed to move to a better location. They traveled west to Indiana, where they established Prophetstown at the fork of the Wabash and Tippecanoe Rivers.

Chapter 4 – The War of 1812

Although Tecumseh and the Prophet (Tenskwatawa) left Ohio, several Shawnee remained. Chief Big Snake and others sent out a declaration of peace and friendship to the people of the United States. However, things remained tenuous between the settlers and Native Americans. In 1806, a large number of Native Americans gathered again at Greenville, apparently to hear the Prophet speak. Many settlers in Ohio believed there was more to the Native American activity than a desire to retain traditional ways; they thought the tribes had been coerced with British gold and promises.

In 1807, the people heard the news of the British ship *Leopard*'s attack on the American vessel *Chesapeake*. There was open speculation in Ohio that the British were also behind the Burr conspiracy. The British Empire had cast a long shadow over America since the end of the Revolutionary War. King George III was frail, blind from cataracts, and suffered from bouts of serious illness, and the British were consistently preoccupied with the Napoleonic Wars at this time. Even so, the British never forgot their former colonies. The Americans were always on guard for another attempt from Britain to retake its former territory. The incident between the *Leopard* and the *Chesapeake* was one in a string of altercations stemming from the habit of British ships boarding American ships and impressing sailors into service for the Royal Navy. The British claimed these sailors were British sailors who had jumped ship and joined American crews, but the

Americans felt this was a step too far.

The *Chesapeake* was believed to have British deserters on board, though the Americans refuted this claim. In response, the Royal Navy in North America had strict orders to stop the *Chesapeake* and conduct a search for deserters. The *Leopard* found her and demanded to be allowed to search her decks. The captain of the *Chesapeake* refused, so the *Leopard* fired, killing three of the *Chesapeake*'s crew and wounding several others. The *Chesapeake* was unable to return fire and surrendered. The British boarded and promptly captured four sailors who they believed to be deserters. Three of them were born in the US, but one was a deserter and hanged. This set in motion a slow escalation of war between the US and the British Empire. In 1811, a US ship fired on an unsuspecting British vessel, killing nine sailors.

Meanwhile, the Prophet was still spreading his message of war against the US, while his brother, Tecumseh, was busy forming alliances with other tribes. Tecumseh had been born near Dayton, Ohio, into a Shawnee tribe that had previously lived in Pennsylvania. He had plenty of experience with the Americans. Supposedly, Tecumseh had at one point courted a white settler's daughter. His vision was to unite all of the Native Americans along the Ohio and Mississippi river valleys into one large confederation that could push the white settlers back across the Appalachians and Alleghenies, thereby reclaiming lost territories.

Just as Tecumseh was working on his confederacy and looking for aid from Great Britain, William Henry Harrison secured three million acres in the Treaty of Fort Wayne, which was signed with the Lenape, Miami, Kickapoo, and Potawatomi. The Shawnee had not been invited.

In 1810, after hearing that Tecumseh denounced the Treaty of Fort Wayne, Harrison invited the Shawnee chief to meet him in Vincennes with thirty warriors. Tecumseh arrived with four hundred warriors and repeated his message about the treachery of the US. Harrison was impressed with the war chief and recognized the threat facing America.

Tecumseh traveled south to secure an alliance with the Creek, and Harrison formed an army and marched toward Prophetstown. The Prophet seized the opportunity and attacked Harrison's army while they were camped near the Tippecanoe River. The Prophet's assurance that the enemy's gunpowder would turn to sand and his bullets to soft mud did not happen, and Harrison's forces were able to win the day in what would be called the Battle of Tippecanoe. Harrison then destroyed Prophetstown.

Tecumseh returned to find his village destroyed and his confederation in shambles. He placed the blame squarely on his brother. This forced his hand and drove him to seek an alliance with the British. In Ohio, the prevailing sentiment was that the British were behind Tippecanoe. They believed the Americans needed to fight for their liberties against the British Empire's oppression.

A group in the federal government spearheaded by Henry Clay of Kentucky pushed for war against Britain. James Madison, Jefferson's handpicked successor, was now president, but he and Congress seemed to waver on the idea of war. The debate was drawn out. The people of Ohio, for the most part, seemed to want war against those they believed were behind Native American aggression. Finally, in June 1812, Madison drafted a declaration of war that only briefly mentioned Native Americans. It mainly focused on maritime issues. The US House of Representatives and the Senate passed the declaration, thus beginning the War of 1812.

Ohio was already well into its preparations. Governor Meigs ordered soldiers to defend Detroit from a possible British attack. Four thousand volunteers and regulars arrived in Dayton with the plan to provide support to the fort in Detroit. Meigs told the Ohio legislature that this war was clearly about the defense of Ohio from Native Americans and their British supporters. Ohio, a place he called the "land of freedom," had been stained with "the blood of her sons." His actions were intended to end the fighting and drive both the Native Americans and the British away from Ohio's territory forever.

Meigs gave command of his army to the governor of Michigan, Brigadier General William Hull. Hull marched from Dayton to Urbana, where his army joined with the Fourth US Infantry under the command of Lieutenant Colonel James Miller. This army trudged through difficult terrain and eventually built a blockhouse at the future sight of Kenton, Ohio. Hull sent much of his personal baggage up the Maumee River aboard the *Cuyahoga*, hoping to lessen the load on his packhorses and help speed his journey to Detroit. This would prove to be folly because among his possessions were detailed accounts of the army and its design to fortify Detroit. These accounts fell into his enemy's hands when the British captured the *Cuyahoga* not long after it left.

Still, Hull reached Detroit in time to take advantage of the general vulnerability of Fort Malden, which sat in Canadian territory. However, he did not attack, instead giving signs that he lacked the fortitude to commence a large-scale attack on the enemy. The British, under the command of Major General Isaac Brock, and the Native Americans, now under the command of Tecumseh, began to harass the Americans by attacking their supply line that ran south from Detroit into Ohio. Hull sent two forces, one larger than the next, to secure his supply line, but both were attacked and beaten back by the allied forces of British and Native Americans. Some of the American soldiers refused to venture onto non-American soil. Hull found himself in a difficult situation, and his previous boasts of liberating Canada now seemed hollow.

After learning of the fall of Fort Mackinac and the slaughter of the people inside Fort Dearborn, near present-day Chicago, Hull was pushed into retreating from his position back to Detroit. Many of the soldiers were opposed to this move, but their complaints went unheard. Brock then began to fire on Fort Detroit, with one shell landing in the officer's mess hall. General Hull quickly surrendered his entire army. The British and Native Americans had squarely defeated the Americans, mostly Ohioans, right on Ohio's doorstep. Things couldn't have seemed worse. Hull was dismissed and brought up on charges of cowardice.

Luckily, Brock and Tecumseh did not pursue an invasion of Ohio. Instead, there was time for the Americans to regroup and gather another force under a new leader. William Henry Harrison, the hero of Tippecanoe, stepped into the vacuum left by Hull. In January 1813, Harrison sent a force of 850 up the Maumee while he continued to train his larger force in the south. This expeditionary force was overwhelmed by the British and Native Americans. Harrison realized that much like the victories at Fallen Timbers and Tippecanoe, the key to success in Ohio would rely on well-trained soldiers who could counter surprise attacks.

However, matters were out of Harrison's hands. Secretary of War John Armstrong ordered Harrison to be on the defense and not to pursue an assault on the British. Thus, Fort Meigs, on the southern shore of the Maumee River near modern-day Perrysburg, became the last bastion of American protection in northern Ohio. The fort was constructed during the 1812/13 winter in harsh conditions. By spring, it had been completed and just in time. Reports began to come in of Native American activity along the Maumee, and Harrison was informed that six thousand British were at Fort Malden, ready to venture south against them. It would turn out that the British, under General Henry Proctor, had only about one thousand men, but they joined with Tecumseh's one thousand warriors and reached Fort Meigs at the end of April.

On May 1ˢᵗ, the British began firing cannons at the fort. Harrison was inside with 1,100 men. The firing continued for four days. Harrison learned that a company of Kentucky riflemen was coming to provide support. He ordered some of them to cross the river and take out the British cannons on the northern shore of the Maumee and then cross back and attack the remaining British and Native American forces, with the rest of their unit attacking them as well. The Kentuckians were successful at taking the cannons but did not follow orders and pursued the British and Native Americans on the northern side. They fell into an ambush, where they were captured and killed. The attack on the remaining forces on the southern side of the river resulted in a stalemate.

Things might have remained this way, except that many of the Native Americans began to leave the fight, as they were unaccustomed to sieges. Also, several Canadian militiamen asked for leave so they could plant their crops for the spring. Proctor was unable to keep his forces together and had to withdraw. Harrison took the opportunity to resupply Fort Meigs from Cincinnati and wait for the next attack. Soldiers were also sent to Cleveland and Fort Stephenson to provide protection.

Proctor returned on July 29ᵗʰ but with fewer men and only one cannon. There were a large number of Native Americans with him, but Harrison was well provisioned and had two thousand men inside the fort. Proctor shelled the fort for eight days, achieving little. Realizing that he could not take the fort and fearing that he was losing the confidence of Tecumseh and his men, he decided to attempt to take a smaller target, Fort Stephenson, which lay on the Sandusky River and is the location of present-day Fremont, Ohio.

Proctor and Tecumseh arrived on August 12th, 1813, with about 1,500 to 2,000 men. The commanding officer at Fort Stephenson was Major George Croghan. Even though he was only t twenty-one-years old, he was already a veteran of the Battle of Tippecanoe. Harrison had ordered him to leave Fort Stephenson, but Croghan convinced the general that it was better to stay. Proctor offered Croghan the chance to surrender the fort without a shot, but Croghan rejected the offer. Inside the fort was only 160 men. The British began to fire at the fort, but the walls held. Wanting to show the Native Americans that the British were offering more than just token gestures, Proctor ordered his men to storm the fort.

Croghan was able to hit the approaching British with a cannon loaded with musket shot. Kentucky sharpshooters took out several more. Two hundred British were killed or wounded. The Native American losses were not recorded, as the bodies were removed at night. The losses were too great, and Proctor ordered a retreat. The attack on Fort Stephenson, which was meant to be an easy display of force, had been a disaster. British soldiers would never again set foot in Ohio. A month later, Commodore Oliver Perry took control of Lake Erie, which meant Proctor could not supply his army via the water. He withdrew his forces from America and returned to Canada.

Tecumseh was enraged, as he felt the Native Americans had once again been abandoned by the British. His people could not retreat so easily.

The British left Fort Detroit, but their retreat was disorganized, and they left behind precious supplies. General Harrison, in the meantime, had an overflow of support in volunteer soldiers from Ohio and Kentucky. He took what men he could and pursued Proctor. He caught up to the British and Native American forces on the Thames River in Ontario, east of Detroit. Harrison had 3,760 soldiers, while Proctor and Tecumseh had an estimated 1,400.

The Americans led with a direct assault from the mounted Kentuckians, who, Harrison reasoned, would be best suited to riding through a forested area. His plan worked, and they were able to capture the British cannons after only one shot. The British were routed, and many fled, including General Proctor.

Tecumseh made his last stand in a nearby swamp. The fighting was severe, but everything fell apart once Tecumseh was killed. The Native Americans began to turn and flee without clear leadership. Tecumseh, who had ravaged the US Armed Forces for many years, had been defeated. His confederation of various Native American tribes began to fall apart almost immediately. The Native Americans felt the British had betrayed them, and the American fear of a British and Native American alliance was now gone.

Harrison withdrew his troops to Detroit instead of pursuing the British or Native Americans, mainly because many of his soldiers' enlistments were about to expire, which would greatly diminish his fighting force. Still, though the Battle of the Thames was not a particularly impressive or large battle, its implications were more definitive. The British were driven out of Ohio for good, by Harrison on land and by the capture of Lake Erie by Perry. The threat of Native American violence in the northwestern corner of the state was all but nullified. The Native Americans would continue their journey westward and continue to battle American expansion in other lands. William Henry Harrison was a national celebrity, and his victories at Tippecanoe and the Thames helped him get into the White House, if only briefly.

Ohio now seemed a much calmer place, but it was not necessarily quieter. The number of businesses and the number of people were growing at an astonishing rate. In 1811, a vessel traveled down the Ohio River unlike any vessel the people of Ohio had seen before. It was called the *New Orleans*, and it was traveling from Pittsburgh to its namesake city. It was propelled not by oars, sails, or the current. It was powered by steam, and it opened up a whole new world for Ohio because goods no longer had to go south to New Orleans and into the Gulf of Mexico. These ships could go upstream with ease. Ships no longer needed a crew of strong oarsmen to struggle up the mighty Ohio. A steamer could glide along at speeds approaching fifteen miles an hour. Times were changing.

Chapter 5 – Progress

The War of 1812 continued after the Battle of the Thames. The British took Washington, DC, and burned the White House in 1814. Yet, in the same year, the war turned against the British. The American forces won the Battle of Plattsburg Bay in Lake Champlain. This led to the signing of the Treaty of Ghent between the British and the Americans, which included terms over the boundaries between the US and Canada and the return of any conquered land. Famously, the news of the peace treaty did not reach the British in the southern US in time, so they went ahead with their attack on New Orleans. The attack was courageously repelled by General Andrew Jackson. So ended the War of 1812.

While peace might seem like the hoped-for outcome to Ohioans, many complained about the sudden absence of military orders for supplies of food, rope, and other things that Ohio produced. There were no armies to sell to, and Ohio faced a sudden loss of many customers. Also, notably, the military often paid in cash, which was helpful in paying off debts. After the war, farmers in Ohio had a scarcity of currency. Gone were the days of paying money for pounds of pork, barrels of wheat, or tons of hemp. By 1817, prices had dropped all across the state. A few years prior, wheat had sold at seventy-five cents per barrel in Cincinnati but now fetched only twenty-five cents per barrel.

This exemplified a larger trend in the rest of the nation. In 1815, Britain and France ended the almost continuous state of war that had existed between the two countries since the late 1600s. While these two countries were at war, the US prospered by trading with both of them. But once peace had been made, US manufactured goods and materials were no longer in high demand.

Since farmers in Ohio could no longer sell their goods, they were no longer able to pay the debt they owed for their land. The federal government and local banks began to demand payment; if they didn't receive it, they repossessed the land. It eventually led to a banking and economic crisis and the first US depression. It would be called the Panic of 1819.

Ohio lawmakers tried to counteract this by levying a tax on the Bank of the United States, hoping they could have money to loan to individuals in danger of losing their land. However, this action was overruled by the Supreme Court. For many people in Ohio who were now poverty-stricken, the enemy was clearly the Bank of the United States. When Andrew Jackson ran for the presidency, he railed against the Bank of the United States, and Ohioans felt like he was one of them.

In 1814, Return Meigs Jr. resigned as governor of Ohio to become postmaster general under President Madison. This meant the speaker of the house, Othniel Looker, became governor for the year. Thomas Worthington, a previous US senator of Ohio, became governor for two terms. Worthington promoted a common school system, the development of a state library, and the building of canals. In 1818 and during the Panic of 1819, the governor was Ethan Allen Brown. Brown's administration devised collecting a tax on the Bank of the United States. The tax was eventually deemed unconstitutional, and the Supreme Court forced Ohio to pay back the over $100,000 it had collected from the federal government. Brown also supported the building of canals. He eventually retired to his home in Rising Sun, Indiana.

Through the 1820s and into the 1830s, Ohio's greatest project was the Ohio and Erie Canal. The Erie Canal, which would connect the markets of New York with those of Lake Erie, began in 1817 and officially opened in 1825. At that time, plans began to build a canal connecting Lake Erie to the Ohio River, thus creating a cross-country water highway. Producers in Ohio could get their products to the East Coast more quickly and at less cost than going over land.

It would take seven years of hard labor to complete the canal. The work was largely done by Irish and German immigrants who had newly arrived in the area. The canal ended in Portsmouth and allowed travel from Cincinnati to Cleveland in about eighty hours, a journey that had previously taken weeks.

The construction of the canal helped bolster Ohio's economy. Flour, which had once sold for ten cents a barrel, now flowed in record numbers out of Cleveland and to the eastern markets for as much as one dollar a barrel. Ohio grain was cheaper and easier to get than any other source, so places like New York and Baltimore bought as much as they could. The canal became something like an artery through the state. It carried iron, oats, coal, cheese, pork, wool, and whiskey out of the state and brought in once prohibitively expensive items like coffee, tea, sugar, and imported china. Middle-class households could enjoy things that had once been exclusive to the very rich. Not just that but ideas also traveled more quickly into Ohio from the east, including fashion, recipes, books, politics, and art.

In 1820, according to census records, Ohio had an estimated population of 581,000 people. It was ranked the fifth-most populous state in the country. By 1830, it had a population of almost a million people and was the fourth-most populous state in the country. Cincinnati became the first western city to break into the top ten largest cities, with a population of 24,831. At that size, the "Queen City," as it was known, dwarfed every other town in the state, none of which were even in the top one hundred most populous cities in the country.

Cincinnati became the primary location for pork-packing in the region. Hogs were brought to market and slaughtered, and pork, bacon, and lard were rendered in the city. There was also a large byproducts industry that developed from pork-packing, such as the manufacturing of soap, glue, candles, shoe polish, buttons, fertilizer, and mattresses. Much of the pork-packing was done in the winter when the meat and lard were less likely to spoil, so farmers, stonemasons, and bricklayers who were idle at that time of year could benefit from seasonal employment. In the winter of 1822/23, for example, Cincinnati processed 2.7 million pounds of meat. Four years later, it processed almost three times as much. Cincinnati overshadowed even Baltimore and was the pork center of the country.

Hogs were often herded through the streets of Cincinnati in the fall, and though residents and travelers complained of the mess and smell, the market continued to grow. As long as people were making a profit, the hogs were a part of city life. Another part of city life in Cincinnati was a structure that seemed to be the subject of ridicule by almost everyone who wrote about it. It was a place called Trollope's Bazaar. This early version of a mini-mall was built in 1826 by Frances Trollope, a British businesswoman. Her bazaar would not last, but perhaps she had the last laugh since she went back to England and wrote a popular book that was highly critical of Cincinnati and Americans in general.

In the 1830s, Cincinnati consisted of buildings chiefly constructed of brick, with the tastes of the time favoring pale bricks. Most of these structures were newly built. The roads were wide and rectangular. The most interesting part of the city was the landing or riverfront area, where commerce and entertainment gave the city an air of vitality. This was a new city making its mark on the world. Some even called it the "Paris of America" due to the gardens and scenic walkways that could be found throughout; these were not in the path of herds of pigs. At night, the streets were unlit, as there were no street lamps at this time, but if one looked into the three-story brick houses, one could see families with as many amenities and styles as one might find on the Atlantic coast.

Starting in 1817, the Native Americans still in Ohio were placed into defined reservations and given instructions on American methods of agriculture. The hope was they would assimilate into white culture. This effort was largely taken up by a group of Ohio Quakers, who volunteered and, at great expense, built mills and schools for the Shawnee. The results were not enough to convince the Native Americans to stay on their land when offers came to buy it. In 1832, the Shawnee of the Wapakoneta and Hog Creek clans left or were removed to Indian Territory west of the Mississippi River.

A group of Methodists attempted the same thing with a group of Wyandots on a reservation at Upper Sandusky. The Native Americans were receptive to the ideas of honesty and kindness, but they could not understand why God would make a book about distant people in distant lands in a language they could not read and why the Methodists attacked their traditional dances and rituals. Still, some of the Wyandots converted over the next decade. Finally, in 1842, the Treaty with the Wyandots removed this last group from Ohio. They, too, went west to Indian Territory.

The frontier had moved past Ohio, and the last vestiges of the great wilderness that the first settlers had encountered were gone. The state's cities and towns were busy and growing. Industry was spreading, and the troubles of the War of 1812 and the Panic of 1819 were long gone for many. Lake Erie, the Miami Valley, and the Sandusky, Scioto, Maumee, Cuyahoga, and Ohio Rivers were bursting with traffic. The year 1836 saw the completion of a new mode of transportation in the state; the Erie and Kalamazoo Railroad line stretched for thirty-three miles and connected Toledo to Adrian, Michigan.

Ohio's governor from 1822 to 1826 was Jeremiah Morrow, a lingering member of the Federalist Party. Under his stewardship, the Erie Canal and many other important canals were completed. He helped establish a state-supported school system. Morrow helped found the Whig Party in Ohio.

Allen Tremble served as governor from 1826 to 1830. He was the last Federalist of note in Ohio politics. However, as governor, he would come to be identified as a National Republican or Anti-Jacksonian, as he allied with Henry Clay and former President John Quincy Adams.

Then came Duncan McArthur, often considered the last of the frontier governors. He served from 1830 to 1832 and was a National Republican or what would become a Whig. MacArthur had been a soldier, fighting under Generals Harmar and Harrison in the so-called "Ohio Indian Wars." During his administration, Ohio saw railroads begin to grow across the state.

There was at least one hiccup to the peace and prosperity that Ohio saw in the 1820s and 1830s: the Toledo War, which began in 1832. Going back to the original plans of the Northwest Territory, the proposed division of states included a border that ran from the bottom tip of Lake Michigan straight east to intersect Lake Erie. This line would be the northern boundaries of Ohio and Indiana.

According to the original maps, the line was above the mouth of the Maumee River. However, the initial maps had been off by a significant amount. According to later surveys, a straight line would pass below the area where the Maumee flowed into Lake Erie.

The matter remained disputed but unimportant until 1832 when Ohio sought to establish a city there named Toledo. The Territory of Michigan, which was trying to become a state, did not care for this move. This small sliver of land was important mainly because of canal traffic that came from Lake Erie, down the Maumee, and into a canal network that connected much of the state. Toledo was a prime location for a city and held great potential for future industries.

The fight over this land was largely political in nature. Several surveys were conducted, with most agreeing that Michigan should have the land. However, Ohio was a state with a large population, and Michigan had little to no power in Washington, DC. Ohio also included the new states of Indiana and Illinois in a bill that defined the boundaries they wanted.

Things escalated, and by 1834, the threat of an armed conflict between Ohio and Michigan became real. The president, Andrew Jackson, was duly concerned and feared the outcome might not only disrupt business in the west but also cause problems in the next election. Ohio was crucial for his second term. Ohio and Michigan called their respective militias to the disputed area in 1835.

Washington quickly responded with a compromise. Michigan would be given its statehood but had to give up its claim to Toledo. Michigan would also be given the Upper Peninsula as part of the state. At the time, this seemed a small concession, but the area proved to be rich in timber, minerals, and majestic scenery. Michigan would officially gain statehood in 1837. Ohio got what it wanted, largely due to its population, economic importance, and Jackson's need to secure a second term.

Ohio's governor during the Toledo War was Robert Lucas, who served from 1832 to 1836. He personally led the Ohio state militia to meet Michigan's governor, Stevens T. Mason, and its territorial militia. Luckily, no fighting actually broke out, and no one was killed. Mason was removed as Michigan's governor, and Ohio was given the Toledo land. Lucas County, which includes Toledo, was named after the governor who helped to secure the land for the state. However, Lucas would not remain in Ohio for long. He became the first governor of Iowa and stayed there after retirement. He died on his Iowa farm in 1853.

The first Whig governor of Ohio was Joseph Vance, who served from 1836 to 1838. Vance followed the tradition of politicians like Henry Clay. He supported the continued building of canals and railroads, favored public schools, was anti-capital punishment, and encouraged abolitionist activity. However, he lost the support of many abolitionists when he submitted to Kentucky's request to extradite John B Mahan, who was suspected of aiding runaway slaves. This action led to Vance's defeat at the end of his first term.

He lost to Wilson Shannon, who served from 1838 to 1840 and then from 1842 to 1844. Shannon was the first governor of Ohio who had been born in the state. Shannon graduated from Ohio University. He was a lawyer and a Democrat. In 1838, he campaigned on bank reform, as banks were issuing large amounts of banknotes that resulted in uncontrolled speculation. He lost the 1840 election to Whig Thomas Corwin but won it back in a rematch in 1842. Shannon went on to serve as a diplomat to Mexico during the build-up to the Mexican-American War. In 1855, he served as the governor of the Territory of Kansas during the time of increased tensions between pro-slavery and anti-slavery Americans in the lead-up to the Civil War.

The year 1851 saw the beginning of construction of the Cincinnati, Hamilton, and Dayton Railroad, or the C H & D RR, nicknamed the "Charge High and Damn Rough Ride" by some passengers. The railroad's main purpose was to carry people between these cities and among the many small cities that were created along its tracks. The first railroad that connected Ohio with the eastern states was the Baltimore and Ohio Railroad or the B & O, which still exists today. This line went through the Appalachian Mountains and allowed passengers and cargo to pass directly between the two regions, sometimes at the alarming and exciting speed of thirty miles per hour. Following the Civil War, railroad production increased significantly in Ohio, and many of the various lines linked up. The C H & D became part of the B & O, and the Little Miami Railroad became a leg of the Pennsylvania Railroad.

In 1850, Cincinnati hosted the first Ohio State Fair, which had been delayed due to a cholera outbreak. Winners at the fair received medals, and the winner of an essay contest about soil improvement was awarded a $50 cash prize. Over the course of two days, the fair, which was agriculturally focused, saw as many as thirty thousand people attend it. In the following year, the fair was held in Cleveland, Dayton, and Newark. It was not until 1886 that the fair found a permanent home at what is now called the Ohio Expo Center in Columbus.

Chapter 6 – Courage

In 1832, a twenty-one-year-old woman named Harriet moved to Cincinnati with her family. Her father had just gotten a job as president of Lane Theological Seminary. She eventually met and fell in love with a man named Calvin Stowe. They married and had six children while living in Ohio. It was there that the woman, known forever as Harriet Beecher Stowe, solidified her opinions on slavery and also suffered heartache that she recognized as being similar to the plight of slaves. After she moved out of Ohio, she wrote and published *Uncle Tom's Cabin*. The book came out in 1852 and became a bestseller. It revealed the brutal reality of slavery and was based largely on research she had conducted on the Underground Railroad in Ohio.

Mordecai Bartley became governor of Ohio in 1844. He was a Whig and sought to repeal the "black laws" that denied rights to African Americans. Bartley's successor was William Bebb, another Whig and former teacher. He served from 1846 to 1849, and though he disagreed with the Mexican-American War, he provided volunteers as requested by the federal government.

The last Whig governor of Ohio was Seabury Ford, who served from 1849 to 1850. His short term was due to a delay in organizing the General Assembly. Under Ford, the black laws were repealed, but a segregation law was put into place. A new constitutional convention was also called to give Ohio a new and more useful constitution.

The Ohio Constitution of 1851 took some of the power away from the Ohio General Assembly. Now, voters had the right to select the governor, other high officials, and judges. The voters also had the task of approving or denying the new constitution, which they approved in large numbers. The Constitution of 1851 did not give women or African Americans the right to vote, but after many amendments, it remains the primary law of the state of Ohio.

The last governor elected under the old 1803 constitution was Reuben Wood, who was a Democrat and vocal about his opposition to slavery and the Fugitive Slave Act. He would become the first governor elected under the new 1851 constitution. He served from 1850 to 1853. He was succeeded by William Medill, a Democrat who served from 1853 until 1856.

The political climate of Ohio was getting heated, as the issue of slavery came to be of greater and greater importance. Medill sought reelection but lost to Salmon P. Chase, who served as the first Republican governor from 1856 to 1860. Chase was openly opposed to slavery and defended former slaves in court. His time as governor was marred by the Panic of 1857 and then by a scandal involving the embezzlement of $550,000 by a former treasurer. Still, Chase would go on to become the secretary of the treasury and then chief justice of the Supreme Court, both nominations by President Abraham Lincoln.

As early as 1815, lines were run in Ohio for what would come to be known as the Underground Railroad. Due to Ohio's proximity to the South and its relatively short distance to Canada, the state became a primary conduit for escaped slaves. Though most people in the state opposed slavery within their borders, only a few took action to provide humanitarian relief and protection to slaves trying to get into Canada.

Since the passing of the federal Fugitive Slave Act, escaped slaves could not simply make it across the Ohio River to be free; they needed to get out of the country altogether. Ohio was the most popular route for these brave men and women to take. Underground Railroad stops lined the Ohio River at Cincinnati, Marietta, Steubenville, Moundsville, Portsmouth, and many more. From these points, slaves could travel a spider web of splitting paths that crisscrossed the state. Eventually, they came to places like

Cleveland, Toledo, Sandusky, Lorain, and so on that provided routes by land and water to the Canadian border.

Operators who harbored runaway slaves were many and varied. A family named Wilson, for instance, operated out of College Hill near Cincinnati. The daughter worked in the city and would receive information about runaway slaves heading to her family's house. Thus, they could prepare and provide food and clothing to these visitors. When fugitive slave hunters were in the area, the former slaves hid in a tiny crawlspace in the attic. The Wilsons only stopped when their activities became too well known and endangered the runaway slaves.

There were an estimated 1,543 operators in Ohio in the years leading up to the Civil War. This was almost as much as the number of operators in every other state combined. Operators were poor, rich, white, and black. Some lived in the countryside, and some lived in the middle of large cities. As many as fifty thousand slaves made their way through Ohio on the Underground Railroad.

In 1855, an escaped slave managed to cross the Ohio River and make his way north until he got to Shelby in north-central Ohio. He had been tracked, so the slave hunters knew he was in town, and they watched every means of exit. The slave hid at an operator's house, but they did not know how they would get him past the hunters. The slave hunters were watching the rail stations, but they never saw the slave they were looking for. They failed to notice the coffin that was being sent north to Sandusky for burial. When the coffin reached Sandusky, it was picked up by another operator, who promptly opened it and let the escaped slave out. He continued on his way to Canada.

In 1851, Akron, Ohio, was the location of the Ohio Women's Rights Convention at Stone Church. There Sojourner Truth, a former slave, delivered her famous "Ain't I a Woman?" speech. (Truth more than likely never used that phrase in her speech, but later writers gave her the speech patterns of Southern slaves, even though she was from New York, and her first language was Dutch.) The speech was published in several forms and used to help recruit soldiers for the American Civil War.

While opinions in Ohio differed on how to solve the problem of slavery or if it was even a problem at all, when the American Civil

War broke out in 1861, it was clear that Ohio would be on the side of the Union. The state sent 300,000 soldiers to fight against the Confederate States of America; the state was only surpassed by New York and Pennsylvania. There were no major battles in the state, but General Ulysses S. Grant and General William Tecumseh Sherman were both from Ohio. Also, the lengthy Confederate raid conducted by General John Hunt Morgan was largely within Ohio.

Morgan commanded the Confederate cavalry and began his longest raid in 1863 into Ohio in the town of Harrison in the southwest. He went east, attempting to disrupt supply lines and distract Federal forces from attacking Robert E. Lee's forces in the east and joining the siege of Vicksburg in Mississippi. Morgan's Raiders, as they were called, did considerable damage and upset the daily lives of many Ohioans, but in the end, the longest raid of the Civil War was considered a failure. Lee lost at Gettysburg, and Grant successfully ended his Vicksburg campaign. Morgan was captured at West Point, Ohio. He was imprisoned in the state penitentiary in Columbus, but he and some of his men managed to escape. He rejoined the Confederate Army and faced a court martial but was killed in battle in 1864.

The Civil War would be Ohio's first brush with not just mortality but also fame. One of the most notable Civil War soldiers from Ohio was Rutherford B. Hayes, who helped form the 23rd Ohio Volunteers and rose to the rank of major general. He helped chase Morgan's Raiders. He would go on to serve as governor of Ohio for three terms and eventually became the nineteenth president of the United States.

Another fellow Ohioan soldier was James A. Garfield, who led a company of the 42nd Ohio Infantry Volunteers. He was also part of the fight against General Morgan. At thirty years old, he became the youngest general in the Union Army and also reached the rank of major general. While still in service, he was elected to US Congress, where he served for seventeen years. He went on to become the twentieth president of the United States. In fact, including Ulysses S. Grant, the eighteenth, nineteenth, and twentieth presidents were all Ohioans, a feat only matched by the state of Virginia.

By the end of the Civil War in 1865, Ohio had become a center for industry and manufacturing. In 1861, Cleveland had its first oil refinery. Four years later, it had thirty refineries, partly thanks to the work of resident John Davison Rockefeller. Rockefeller took advantage of high prices in oil but also used ways to use the byproducts of oil refining to sell petroleum jelly, gasoline, and paraffin wax. His business acumen led to him becoming the wealthiest man in the US.

At around the same time, Columbus was becoming more than just the state's capital. Due to its central location, the city became a center for industry. It was one of the largest producers of wagons, carriages, and buggies. It also became home to the Ohio Agricultural and Mechanical College in 1873, which would be renamed Ohio State University. Also, in the 1870s, Dayton became a large manufacturer of paper, brass works, lumber, and boxcars. Toledo joined Cleveland as a site for oil refining and became home to several glassmaking factories.

In 1850, Robert Bell opened a shoe factory in Portsmouth; at the time, all shoes were made by hand. In 1869, Bell purchased a machine that could make two hundred shoes per day. This began a boom in shoe production that would lead to Portsmouth being named the "Shoe Capital of the World."

Youngstown became a center for iron production, and one of the industrialists who made their fortune there was David Tod. Tod was elected governor in 1861 and served from 1862 until 1864. He was a member of the newly formed National Union Party, which was an attempt to combine Republicans and pro-Union Democrats. John Brough, who was from Marietta and the owner of *The Cincinnati Enquirer*, secured the Union Party's nomination after Tod's disappointing term.

Brough helped with the war effort but died of a stroke four months before the end of his term. His lieutenant governor, Charles Anderson, finished his term and supported amnesty at the end of the Civil War. Jacob Cox, a Union Party nominee, was governor from 1866 to 1868. His term was not noteworthy except for the fact that, as a fervent abolitionist, he surprised some with his equally strong feelings about denying blacks the right to vote and instituting segregation throughout the state.

Rutherford B. Hayes was born in Delaware, Ohio, in 1822 and became the nineteenth president of the United States.

Rutherford B. Hayes was the governor from 1868 to 1872 and then again from 1876 to 1877. Hayes left his post only to become president of the United States. Between Hayes's second and third terms, Edward F. Noyes served as governor. Like Hayes and many other governors, he practiced law in Cincinnati, where he gained experience and attention. Noyes was a Republican and Civil War veteran who had lost his lower leg during the war. Noyes lost reelection to William Allen, a seventy-year-old Democrat who was brought to office due to economic hardships caused by the Panic of 1873.

Allen's term was unremarkable. He was followed by Hayes, who was then followed by Democrat Richard M. Bishop. Bishop's term became known as problematic largely because he allowed one of his sons to have too much power in granting pardons of convicts. In 1879, Bishop was unable to get renominated by his own party.

The Cincinnati Red Stockings became the country's first professional baseball team in 1869. The team went on to be part of the National League in 1876 but was thrown out because they played games on Sundays and sold beer at their games. The Reds, as they would be called, reformed and joined the more liberal American Association in 1881, which was known for allowing beer sales at games. They returned to the National League in 1890 but were still able to play on Sundays and sell beer at their games.

Near the city of Ashtabula on Lake Erie in December of 1876, a train pulling three passenger cars crossed an iron bridge that collapsed. The train and passengers plummeted sixty feet into a creek. The lamps and furnaces caught the wreckage on fire. Eighty-three people lost their lives, and sixty suffered serious injuries. While this accident was newsworthy, it was not particularly surprising. By this time, Ohio was crisscrossed with thousands of miles of rail lines. The tracks were often constructed quickly and cheaply so railroad companies could maximize profit. Railroad accidents occurred with increased frequency at the end of the 19th century. The Ashtabula train wreck did not cause any immediate changes in railroad policy. Railroads had become the most cost-effective means of moving cargo and people around the state.

James A. Garfield was born in Moreland Hills, Ohio, and was assassinated in 1881.

In 1880, James A. Garfield was elected the twentieth president of the United States. He had been born in a log cabin in Orange Township in northeastern Ohio in 1831. Garfield joined the Republican Party and was part of what was called the "spoils system" of politics. The leader of the spoils system was Senator Roscoe Conkling of New York. The faction of the Republican Party that favored the spoils system and sided with Conkling was known as the Stalwarts. Conkling was opposed by Senator James Blaine of Maine, who sought to end the patronage of the spoils system. Patronage allowed federal politicians to place friends and relatives in important government positions, thus ensuring their loyalty. Blaine's side was known as the Half-Breeds. Rutherford B. Hayes, who served before Garfield, was a Half-Breed.

Garfield's nomination was a surprise to everyone, including himself. He was a compromise candidate who had the respect of both the Stalwarts and the Half-Breeds. To ensure the Stalwarts would support him, Garfield made Chester A. Arthur, a Stalwart, his vice president. Garfield won the election and then made Senator Blaine his secretary of state. The Stalwarts felt betrayed, and Conkling resigned to protest, believing he would be quickly reappointed. This did not happen, so Garfield seemed to have won the battle.

Unbeknownst to everyone involved, a mentally deranged man named Charles Guiteau had become obsessed with the race and, on one occasion, had been allowed to give a confusing speech in support of Garfield. Guiteau considered himself a Stalwart and hoped for a lucrative appointment in the government. He, too, felt betrayed by Garfield.

Guiteau shot and killed the president only a few months into his term. This put Chester A. Arthur into the Oval Office, but Guiteau was once again disappointed when Arthur did not award him a position. Instead, he was captured, tried, and hung as a murderer.

While Garfield's time in office was cut short, the spoils system was on its way out. Garfield would not be the last president from Ohio, nor would he be the last Ohio president to be assassinated.

Chapter 7 – Prosperity

In 1869, Benjamin Franklin Goodrich was convinced by the Akron Board of Trade to move his small rubber factory from New York to Ohio. Akron had only just been incorporated as a city, but like many cities in Ohio, it was forward-thinking and interested in the expansion of industry. The factory began by making fire hoses, beer tubing, and machine belting. Then known as the BF Goodrich Company, it became successful in 1874, mainly due to the increased demand for bicycle tires. Legend has it that Goodrich saw a friend's house burn down in winter and watched as the fire hoses froze and cracked. He then had his hoses embedded with cotton to resist freezing.

The Factories of The B. F. Goodrich Co., Akron, Ohio. Largest Rubber Plant in the World. Two Miles around the grounds. 15,000 Employees. Seventy-Five Acres of Floor Space.

A postcard of the Goodrich factories.

Brothers Frank and Charles Seiberling founded the Goodyear Tire & Rubber Company in Akron in 1898. The company was named after Charles Goodyear, one of the inventors of vulcanized rubber. Goodyear Tire began by making carriage tires, bicycle tires, horseshoe pads, and other rubber items in November of that year. The next year, it began making automobile tires. Companies like Firestone and General Tires were also founded in Akron, making the city the "Rubber Capital of the World."

Cleveland was fast becoming an industrial powerhouse by the end of the 19th century. Part of this was due to a single individual who began his professional career as an unassuming assistant bookkeeper in 1855. John D. Rockefeller was only twenty years old when he started his first business. He transitioned into the oil industry in 1863. In 1870, he started Standard Oil. He was the largest stockholder in this corporation; in 1905, it was worth over a trillion dollars in today's money! Rockefeller was noted for buying underperforming oil refineries and improving their efficiency so they turned a profit. In 1872, Standard Oil bought twenty-two of its twenty-six competitors in Cleveland. Rockefeller organized deals for reduced rates with railroads, and when those were not to his liking, he tried to take control of the railroads himself. He was cutthroat, but he treated his employees well.

By 1880, Rockefeller's net worth was eighteen million dollars; fifty years later, he was worth over a billion dollars. Rockefeller is believed to be the richest person in American history. Standard Oil became the prime example of a modern monopoly. At the same time, Rockefeller gave a considerable amount to his chosen charities and causes. He gave $1.35 million in donations in 1892 alone. He donated to many Cleveland institutions, including the Western Reserve Historical Society, the Ragged School, Bethel Union, the Visiting Nurse Association of Cleveland, and the Dorcas Invalid Home. Many of Cleveland's parks were built on lands donated by Rockefeller.

Early in the year 1884, a man named Kirk sold a horse in Cincinnati. In the hopes of taking his newly earned cash, two men who worked for Kirk, one a man named Berner and the other an unnamed African American, killed him. The murder was discovered, and the murderers were arrested. Berner went to trial and was found guilty only of manslaughter; the judge gave him the maximum sentence of twenty years. However, the people of Cincinnati were furious with the verdict, and what started as a protest turned into a riot.

For several days and nights, the Cincinnati Courthouse riots raged through the streets. Berner was put in the penitentiary in Columbus, but by then, the mob was out of control. The state militia was called in, and the riot took on the semblance of a battle when armed rioters began exchanging fire with the militia. The courthouse in Cincinnati was overrun and burned to the ground. Hundreds of people died in the chaos. Eventually, order was restored as more troops, professional and volunteer, arrived on the scene. A nighttime curfew was enacted for the whole city.

Another Ohioan, Benjamin Harrison, became the twenty-third president of the United States in 1889. Harrison was the grandson of William Henry Harrison. Born on a farm near the Ohio River, Harrison went to Miami University in Oxford, Ohio. He then moved to Indianapolis, where he became involved in politics, eventually becoming a senator. As president, he signed the Sherman Antitrust Act, which hoped to protect people against monopolies like that enjoyed by Rockefeller's Standard Oil.

In the 1880s, Herbert Henry Dow became interested in brines. After he graduated from the Case School of Applied Science (now the Case Western University) in Cleveland, he developed a method for extracting bromine from brine, which could be found in mineral wells in Ohio and Michigan. Bromine was a sought-after chemical used in medicines and photography. He started the Midland Chemical Company in Midland, Michigan, in 1890 and perfected his method of extracting bromine using electrolysis. Dow saw the potential to use this same method, the "Dow method," to extract other chemicals.

However, his financial backers did not support him, and Dow was forced out of Midland Chemical Company. He was unphased by this and created the Dow Chemical Company. Dow began to create bleach powder from sodium hydroxide and chlorine using his method. It was a great success, and Dow Chemical went on to purchase Dow's old business, Midland Chemical Company. His company, Dow Chemical, continues to be a world leader in the chemical industry.

In Dayton, John H. Patterson formed the National Cash Register Company in 1884. Patterson was a pioneer in management, creating factories with large windows that let in light and fresh air. He also hired John Olmsted to landscape the grounds around his factory. Sweat factories were the norm, so Patterson's factory was a breath of fresh air—literally. The NCR became a successful company, and Patterson created a sales training school that trained some of the most successful businessmen of the era, including Thomas Watson Sr., who went on to manage the Computing Tabulating Recording Company, which would become IBM. The NCR also hired Charles F. Kettering, the founder of Delco and head of research for General Motors.

Patterson was regarded as something of an eccentric. He was very health-conscious and was known to have periodic weigh-ins for his employees. If they were underweight, they were given free malted milk. Patterson also became well known for his firing practices. According to legend, on one occasion, an NCR executive arrived to find his desk and belongings being set on fire outside his office. Another rumor says Patterson took his accounting department on a tour of one of his factories. To demonstrate to them how the boiler worked, he burned their ledgers and fired the entire department.

However, Patterson was known to care for his employee. Besides the large windows and landscaping, he also instituted lunchtime lectures, increased wages, and became one of the first industrialists to be concerned with his workers' safety. Patterson and the NCR played a pivotal role in the wake of the devastating 1913 flood in Dayton. NCR factories stopped making registers and made boats for rescuing people stranded in their homes. The factories also provided shelter and food for anyone displaced by the waters.

A new product could be found in stores in the 1880s: an inexpensive soap called Ivory. Procter & Gamble was founded in Cincinnati back in 1837 by William Procter and James Gamble, a candle maker and soap maker, respectively. Both men were immigrants, and their company became very successful throughout the 19th century. They became famous at the end of the century for their new Ivory soap and went on to produce thirty different kinds of soap in their massive factory in what became known as Ivorydale.

The company continued to expand its range of products. P&G, as they were known, made Crisco, Tide laundry detergent, Prell shampoo, Crest fluoride toothpaste, Downy fabric softener, and Pampers disposable diapers, to name a few products. P&G, which is still headquartered in Cincinnati, is a world leader in domestic products and a true household name worth billions of dollars. Today, P&G includes brand names like Vicks, Old Spice, Folgers, Charmin, Bounty, Puffs, Gillette, Pantene, Dawn, Febreze, and Olay.

With the development of factories and industries in Ohio came a shift in the way of living for most Ohioans. No longer were Buckeyes predominantly living on farms; they now lived in cities and worked in factories and offices. This meant a change in the role of the family. Specifically, parents could no longer give their children land to farm and live on with their own families. Children now had to, at least for the most part, make their own way once they reached adulthood. For some, this was an opportunity to climb up the social ladder and make a name for themselves like some of the previously mentioned industrialists. But for many, this meant a future of backbreaking factory work with long hours and little reward.

Poverty was a constant problem in Ohio's larger cities. Many cities created poorhouses and orphanages for families that needed assistance. Local governments often couldn't afford to provide welfare or what was then called "relief" to those living under the poverty line. The Cincinnati Orphan Asylum, founded in the 1830s, typically housed children with living parents who could not afford to take care of their children.

It has been observed that while the fathers of households typically earned most of the family's income in the late 19th century, the wives and children provided almost half of the total income with supplemental work. Thus, families that gave up their children due to poverty were doing so most likely to save the child and not because the child was any sort of burden.

Due to the transition from skilled labor in the earlier part of the century to unskilled labor in the factories in the late 1800s, wages fell. However, the number of salaried or white-collar workers increased during this time and saw an increase in wages. This imbalance helped to fuel the growth of unions in Ohio. The working class in many Ohio cities was often divided on immigrant status, religion, and country of origin. Northern European Protestants and Irish Catholics, who had arrived in the mid-19th century, were often opposed to Jewish and southern or eastern European immigrants, who had arrived late in the century. There was also antagonism between those of European descent and African Americans, some of whom were descended from slaves who had migrated north for better job opportunities.

While some people were engaged in legitimate businesses to become wealthy, there was another way to earn money in Ohio's cities. Peddling, trading services, bartering, and petty and organized crime led to the rise of crime rates. The existence of the poor and the criminal class prompted Ohio's cities to expand their welfare systems and law enforcement. Modernized penitentiaries were built in the hopes of reforming criminals through hard work.

Yet, most of this was not enough to deal with these growing issues. Consequently, many cities simply ignored the problem. In 1896, for example, it was widely known that prostitution was tolerated in Cincinnati provided brothels remained in designated areas. This was true for many other cities in Ohio, including the growing metropolis of Cleveland.

Cleveland, thanks in large part to its growing industries, was becoming the largest city in the state, overtaking Cincinnati in 1900 with over 381,000 residents. One in ten Ohioans was a Clevelander. Both Cleveland and Cincinnati experienced a high population density at the end of the 19th century. Cleveland's Central Area, between Woodland and Cedar Avenues, had almost one hundred people per acre. Cincinnati's West Side neighborhood housed sixty thousand people in a small strip of land close to the Ohio River.

The primary feature of these neighborhoods was cheaply constructed tenements where people struggled to be fed and often lived in cramped and unsanitary conditions. Disease and crime ran rampant there, and little was done to improve these conditions. Still, people flocked to these cities. During the 1880s and 1890s, a large number of immigrants from Hungary, Slovakia, Slovenia, Italy, Greece, and other eastern and southern European countries came in large numbers.

Charles Foster, born in Seneca County, became governor of Ohio in 1880 and served until 1884. Foster, a Republican, was outspoken against the liquor industry and helped to institute heavier taxes and regulations. These policies became unpopular and led to a Democrat victory for George Hoadly in 1883. However, Hoadly was seen as weak and ineffective largely because of his delayed response to the Cincinnati Courthouse riots.

Hoadly was succeeded by Republican Joseph Foraker, who served from 1886 to 1890. Foraker ran not only against Republican candidates but also candidates from the Prohibition, Greenback, and Union Labor Parties. Foraker helped pass regulations on liquor traffic and election reform and established the Ohio Board of Health. After his time as governor, Foraker became a US senator. William Randolph Hearst revealed that Foraker had once accepted $29,500 from Standard Oil. While Foraker claimed it was for legal services, the scandal was enough to force him into retirement.

James E. Campbell served as governor from 1890 to 1892. Campbell's time in office was largely uneventful, though the legislature did pass a law requiring children to attend school for a certain amount of time and labor laws to protect Ohio's workers.

Campbell was defeated for reelection in 1891 by William McKinley, a rising star in Ohio politics.

McKinley was supported by Marcus A. Hanna, a political boss and millionaire. Hanna had gone to high school with John D. Rockefeller in Cleveland and made his first million by the time he was forty years old. McKinley and Hanna had met some time before and had become friends. Hanna saw another possible president from Ohio in McKinley, and becoming governor was a step on that path.

Though times were hard in the wake of the Panic of 1893, McKinley won two terms and would go on to become president of the United States. He was succeeded by Asa Bushnell, another Republican. Bushnell served two terms. Under his administration, the state began to use the electric chair instead of the noose for executions, and the state government also improved working conditions for women and regulated child labor. In 1897, Bushnell won a packed race against candidates from the Democrat, Prohibition, People's, Socialist Labor, Liberty, National Democrat, and Negro Protection parties.

The end of the 19th century saw a drastic change in the makeup of life in Ohio. The great and wealthy industrialists and businessmen used their fortunes to influence policies and politics in the state. Some of these men became known as city bosses. Guy G. Major ran Toledo, and Joseph E. Lowes was the Republican boss of Dayton. While Republican Marcus Hanna was the boss of Cleveland, its rival city of Cincinnati was run by Democrat John R. McLean, who owned *The Cincinnati Enquirer*. The city was also run by Republican bosses Joseph Foraker, the governor and senator, and George B. Cox.

Cox was the son of an English immigrant and was born into a low class. He received little education as a child and worked to help support his family. He eventually saved enough money to buy a bar in Cincinnati at a place called "Dead Man's Corner." He eventually ran for city council, supposedly to stop police raids on his bar. Democrats controlled the city at the time, but Cox was able to win the election, and the raids on his bar immediately stopped.

Although Cox found he had a liking for politics, he only served two terms on the city council. He did help put others into office, though. He gained support from the working class, and they would vote for whatever candidate he supported. Once the candidates were in office, they placed loyal Cox followers in various city positions, from policemen and firefighters to secretaries and even street cleaners. By the end of the century, Cox controlled almost the entire city.

Cox engaged in voter fraud, paying residents of other states to come to Ohio and vote or paying voters to cast more than one ballot under an assumed name. Of course, they always voted for the candidate Cox wanted. It was not until the next century that Cox's power began to fail apart, as the city annexed more neighborhoods with voters that Cox couldn't control.

The Republicans were largely in control of Ohio during this period, while the Democrats only gained some offices for a short amount of time. There were no restrictions on the use of money in politics, so cash was used to buy loyalty and votes. The Republican Party's organization was a massive machine that concerned itself with national issues but was controlled street by street in Ohio towns and cities. The Democrats, on the other hand, were largely unorganized at this time. It was not until 1902 that the Democrats had a permanent headquarters in Columbus.

During this time of corruption and social inequality, the Progressive movement began to grow in the country. Samuel Jones, the mayor of Toledo in 1897, began to gain attention for his anti-corruption actions. Democrat Tom L. Johnson was elected mayor of Cleveland in 1902. Both mayors enacted measures that encouraged civil reform, business regulations, home rule for cities, and city ownership of utilities.

One key element of the reforms in Ohio was the push to change the way in which senators were elected. For the entire history of the state, senators had been appointed by the state legislature, but now, reform-minded progressives felt citizens should vote for the senators who would represent their state in Washington, DC. The Democrats officially endorsed this platform in 1905.

By that time, Republican and Ohioan William McKinley had been elected the twenty-fifth president of the United States. However, in 1901, he was killed by an assassin's bullet at the Pan-American Exposition in Buffalo, New York. The assassin, Leon

Czolgosz, had been ruined in the Panic of 1893 and became an anarchist. He saw McKinley, the product of a political boss and promoter of American expansionism, as a symbol of oppression and felt that it was his duty to kill the president.

McKinley was succeeded by vice president Theodore Roosevelt. Czolgosz was captured and sentenced to death via the electric chair. Because of McKinley's assassination, Congress passed legislation that officially gave the Secret Service the duty of protecting the president.

William McKinley was the second Ohioan president killed by an assassin.
https://en.wikipedia.org/wiki/File:McKinley_(cropped).jpg

Chapter 8 – A New Century

According to the 1900 census, Ohio still had two of the top ten most populated cities. Cleveland was seventh, and Cincinnati was tenth. Chicago was the second-largest city in America with over a million residents; New York was first and boasted almost three and a half million people. It was the last time Cincinnati appeared in the top ten. By 1910, Cleveland was the sixth-largest city, with 560,663 people. St. Louis was still bigger than Cleveland, and Pittsburgh, Detroit, and Buffalo were all in the top ten for the first time. Cincinnati, the home of the riverboat and the pork market, was unable to keep up with the massive industrial growth of the other cities built around oil and steel. Cleveland was a different story.

By 1920, Cleveland was still growing and was the fifth-largest city in America, beating St Louis but overshadowed by Detroit, which sat at number four. The automobile industry was in full swing, after all. In 1920, Los Angeles made its first appearance in the top ten, a sign of things to come. Ten years later, Los Angeles was the fifth-most populous city, and Cleveland had fallen back to sixth. This does not adequately demonstrate the unbelievable growth that cities like Los Angeles saw in the early 20th century. In 1920, LA had a population of 576,673. In 1930, LA more than doubled in size. This is not to say that Ohio was stagnant. For the most part, cities continued to grow, and life took on new dimensions due to the changes of the new century.

The year 1903 was the centennial anniversary of Ohio becoming a state. Ohio had begun with a population of a little over forty-five thousand people, and in 1900, it had a population of over four million. When the state began, the population was completely rural; a hundred years later, it was about 50 percent rural and 50 percent urban. The first state legislature had met in a small building in Chillicothe. A hundred years later, they met in a large state building in the capital of Columbus. The dawn of the 20th century revealed that Ohio would need to adapt.

There was a hint of change in 1896 when Catherine Hitchcock Tilden became the first woman elected to public office in Ohio as a member of the Cleveland Board of Education. For a long time, women had been increasingly involved in social issues, especially the temperance movement. In the 1870s, there was the so-called "Women's Crusade" in Ohio, where a group of women inspired by Dr. Dio Lewis went to saloons and bars to pray for the people there and ask the barkeepers to stop selling alcohol. This was no simple task, as places like Xenia in southwestern Ohio had well over a hundred saloons. It is unclear how many saloons actually closed due to the crusade, but at least one, a place called the Shades of Death, was convinced to stop business by the protesters.

In the realm of women's suffrage, Harriet Taylor Upton of Warren, Ohio, became a nationally recognized proponent. Her father, Ezra B. Taylor, became a congressman in 1880, and Harriet accompanied him to Washington, where she became well known for her intelligence and wit. She was mentored by Susan B. Anthony and joined the National American Woman Suffrage Association, which was headquartered at her house in Warren from 1903 to 1910. Upton became friends with Presidents Hayes, Garfield, McKinley, Harding, and Hoover during her long life. She saw the passage of the Nineteenth Amendment, which allowed women to vote, in 1920, though Ohio had passed a law giving women the vote in the same year just in case the amendment was not ratified in time. Upton died in 1945 at the age of ninety.

From 1900 to 1920, women's suffrage organizations were formed all across the state. A referendum was put on the ballot in 1912 to add an amendment to the Ohio Constitution giving women the right to vote, but the referendum did not pass. However, cities were given the right to allow women voters within their municipalities. In 1916, East Cleveland, a suburb of Cleveland, passed an amendment allowing women to vote in city elections. Governor James M. Cox signed the Reynolds Bill to allow women to vote in presidential elections, but a voter referendum stopped it from becoming law in 1917. However, less than two years later, Ohio ratified the Nineteenth Amendment to the US Constitution, and women gained universal suffrage in the state. It took another three years to have the phrase "white male" removed from the Ohio Constitution as the description of a voter.

Meanwhile, another Ohioan had found himself, albeit uncomfortably, as president of the United States. William Howard Taft was from a well-known family in Cincinnati and made his name in Ohio as a judge on the Cincinnati Superior Court. He accepted a position from Benjamin Harrison to be solicitor general. He was then picked by McKinley to be the chief civil administrator in the newly acquired Philippines after the Spanish-American War; he eventually became governor of the islands. He was considered largely successful in this post. Then, Theodore Roosevelt made him secretary of war and eventually chose him to be his appointed successor.

Taft hated campaigning but won the election and became the twenty-seventh president. He was the seventh president from Ohio after William Henry Harrison, Ulysses S. Grant, Rutherford B. Hayes, James A. Garfield, Benjamin Harrison, and William McKinley. Benjamin Harrison was born in Ohio but made his name in Indiana.

Taft had a general distaste for White House politics. He tried to continue Roosevelt's programs by pursuing more antitrust suits than the previous administration, and he oversaw the breaking up of Rockefeller's Standard Oil monopoly. Taft's administration created the Department of Labor as well. However, he angered many progressives, including Roosevelt, because he kept high tariffs, undermined conservation efforts, and was influenced by corporate money. In 1912, Taft was challenged by Democrat Woodrow Wilson and his old mentor Theodore Roosevelt, who split the Republican vote. Wilson won the election. However, Taft would be appointed chief justice of the Supreme Court, a role that suited him much better.

A gathering of blacks and whites in New York established the National Association for the Advancement of Colored People (NAACP) in 1910. This organization looked to end segregation, establish equal civil rights for African Americans, and end racial violence such as lynchings. The NAACP was active in Ohio from its inception. In 1915, the Columbus branch of the NAACP was formed and immediately worked on getting oppressive police officers removed from their positions. It also tried to keep the film *Birth of a Nation* from being shown in the state. In 1919, the NAACP investigated the cases of black soldiers who were discriminated against in camps, on trains, in their hometowns, in hospitals, and even by the Red Cross. This was during both the build-up of and US involvement in World War I. A large training camp was built near Chillicothe called Camp Sherman.

Camp Sherman was a large training camp in Chillicothe for soldiers in WWI.
https://commons.wikimedia.org/wiki/File:Recruits,_Camp_Sherman,_Ohio._-_NARA_-_533612.tif

Camp Sherman was built in only a few months. The construction of some two thousand buildings led to ancient Native American earthen mounds being bulldozed. At the time, no one seemed to care or notice. The camp's library was unique in that it was not segregated; black and white soldiers could enjoy books in the same place. There was a total of eleven YMCAs (Young Men's Christian Association) built in the camp, with one specifically for African

Americans. However, all the YMCAs were open to people of any color.

The camp was finally decommissioned in 1921, almost three years after the end of the war. The African American 813th Pioneer Infantry regiment trained at Camp Sherman and fought in France in 1918. In that same year, approximately 1,200 soldiers died at the camp due to the influenza epidemic.

As early as 1915, companies in the North, including Ohio, sent recruiters to the South to get African American laborers to migrate for better employment. Southern blacks found they could make as much as two dollars more a day at factories and mills in the North. This was a significant increase since they were making about two dollars a day at rural jobs in the South. This began what would be called the Great Migration. One place that saw this increase in African American laborers was Springfield, Ohio, which is northeast of Dayton.

Springfield's growing black population created tensions within the largely white community. African American veterans of WWI returned home, victors of a foreign war, but many whites felt the blacks needed to be put back in their place since they were deemed inferior. The Ku Klux Klan (KKK) had been reestablished, and membership soared, especially in Indiana and Ohio, which had higher membership numbers than some southern states. Added to this was the fact that with the end of the war, Springfield's employment opportunities decreased, and the economy began to scale back. This created competition for jobs, especially between unskilled white and black workers.

Springfield was also home to the International Harvester Company, a large truck- and harvester-making corporation. In 1912, as part of an antitrust suit, International Harvester was declared a monopoly and worked out an agreement to stop making harvesters completely and only make trucks. This meant the loss of more jobs in Springfield. The summer of 1919 saw a wave of race riots and lynchings all across America. In reaction to this climate, African Americans in Springfield decided to arm and train themselves in case whites decided to attack their businesses, homes, and persons. An undertaker named Patterson, who could pass for white, purchased a large stock of rifles, and WWI veterans began to train blacks on how to defend themselves.

In 1921, the *Springfield Review* published a story about a young white girl who had been attacked by an unknown adult black man. A doctor gave his opinion that he had doubts the girl would recover from her injuries. Rumors began to fly, and crowds gathered in search of the unknown black assailant. After two days, the crowds decided the black community was harboring the assailant, so they descended on the black neighborhood of Springfield. The people of this community got word of the approaching mob and prepared for a fight. They did not get their rifles at first, instead telling the whites they did not have the assailant and that the whites should leave them alone.

Police arrived and approached the African American crowd, telling them to disperse and go home. By that point, some of the African Americans had arrived armed with rifles. They shot a white police officer. This led to the white mob growing to a thousand or more men. However, they were unable to enter the black neighborhood, as they were driven back by gunfire. The African American men repeatedly told police that they were protecting their homes and that they would take care of their part of town. Any whites looking to enter the neighborhood were turned back, often at gunpoint. Eventually, the National Guard was called in. Soldiers armed with machine guns dispersed the white mob. The African Americans left their positions and returned home. Unfortunately, this was not the end of racial violence in Ohio.

Warren G. Harding was born near Blooming Grove, Ohio, but grew up in Caledonia, which is also in Ohio. At seventeen years of age, he moved with his family to Marion, where he bought a newspaper. It became successful enough that Harding bought *The Marion Star* newspaper and became chief editor.

Eventually, Harding entered politics and became a US senator. He then ran for president, partly on a platform of what he called "Americanism," which seemed to be a form of nationalism and isolationism. Harding believed America should take care of issues at home before getting involved in another foreign war. He is often remembered for his call to "normalcy," which resonated with voters after the First World War. Harding decidedly won the 1920 election and became the twenty-ninth president of the United States and the eighth president from Ohio.

The year 1920 also saw the passing of the Volstead Act and the Eighteenth Amendment, which outlawed the sale and production of most alcohol in the country. Prohibition had begun. This opened the door to organized crime. In Cincinnati, lawyer-turned-bootlegger George Remus created an empire selling bonded whiskey from Kentucky. He famously murdered his wife for having an affair and then got himself acquitted with a plea of temporary insanity.

In Cleveland, things were even deadlier. Organized crime in Cleveland began in earnest when the Lonardo brothers and the Porrello brothers immigrated from Sicily. Joseph Lonardo became the Cleveland crime family's first boss and controlled the flow of liquor, but tensions between the brothers rose in 1926 since the Porrellos wanted a larger piece of the business. The next year, two gunmen killed Joseph and John Lonardo, and Joe Porrello became the new boss. Eventually, the Cleveland Syndicate ran all crime in the city and joined with the National Crime Syndicate to become part of the American Mafia. Even after Prohibition was repealed in 1933, organized crime in Ohio continued.

In 1929, the Great Depression began in the US. Ohioans were hit especially hard. Forty percent of factory workers and 67 percent of construction workers lost their jobs. Ohio's unemployment rate reached a staggering 37.2 percent in 1932. Under Franklin Delano Roosevelt's government, programs like the Works Progress Administration (WPA) put some Ohioans back to work in a variety of tasks, including constructing government buildings and creating roads and shelters in parks. Still, Ohio did not see a clear improvement until the demand for jobs once again rose due to World War II.

The Ohio River had always been prone to flooding, but nothing prepared the people who lived along its banks for the flood of 1937. In Cincinnati, the river gauge measured eighty feet, the highest in its history. WPA workers were sent to assist in helping the flood victims, and the federal government sent a fleet from the Army Corps of Engineers and much-needed supplies to the stricken areas. One hundred thousand people were rendered homeless in Cincinnati alone. The citizens opened the floodgates of

Portsmouth, which flooded the business district by ten feet but saved many residences. Ohio was not alone. Areas in Indiana, Kentucky, West Virginia, and Illinois saw large amounts of flooding as well. January 1937 remains the wettest month in recorded history for many areas along the Ohio River.

After the attack on Pearl Harbor, America became involved in World War II. About 12 percent of Ohio's population (839,000 people) joined the fight directly, while many worked at home to assist the soldiers in Europe and the Pacific. Willys-Overland Company in Toledo made Jeeps, while Goodyear in Akron helped with aircraft production. For most Ohioans, the war was a distant concern, but the new jobs and improving economy were reasons to celebrate. However, for the families of the twenty-three thousand men and women who never returned from the war, it was a time of great loss. Those Ohioans, like the soldiers in the Civil War and the soldiers in World War I, had lost their lives in defense of their country and were seen as honoring their great state.

Chapter 9 – A Modern Path

After the end of World War II, most people in Ohio felt the greatest threat to the country was the Soviet Union and, in more general terms, communism. The fight against communism was not like the world wars that were fought on foreign soil, as the people felt the threat was there in the United States in the form of communist spies and agitators.

In 1951, the Ohio General Assembly created the Ohio Un-American Activities Commission (OUAC) to find and arrest any communist agents in the state. The OUAC conducted a series of interviews with supposed communists, most of which were considered "unfriendly" witnesses. The witnesses were asked whether they had been to a certain Communist Party banquet or if they knew another suspected communist. Many answered question after question with the same statement: "I decline to answer the question according to my constitutional right." The OUAC was typically a committee of frustrated interviewers. Still, forty people were indicted, and fifteen were convicted of supporting communism, which was a crime at the time.

The OUAC contended that it had only scratched the surface, estimating that there were 1,300 Communist Party members in the state. The OUAC continued for several more years, but support waned since there were no large numbers of arrests. It became apparent the commission's actions violated one of the core principles of the state: civil liberties.

Ohioans were concerned with the influence of communists, but they were also concerned with civil rights. Many white Ohioans believed racial inequality could prove a hindrance in the Cold War against the Soviet Union. But more importantly, the larger number of black voters from the Great Migration meant civil rights were an increasingly important issue the state government needed to address. With this in mind and thanks to the hard work of civil rights activists, Ohio passed the Ohio Civil Rights Act of 1959, which sought to prevent and eliminate discrimination due to race, color, religion, national origin, or ancestry. It also guaranteed equal access to public facilities and private businesses. Segregation ended at the federal level with *Brown v. Board of Education* in 1954, but this provided additional security at the state level. Also, the 1959 act created the Ohio Civil Rights Commission. While Ohioans were fighting for equal rights, they were also looking to go beyond the limits of the planet.

Born in 1921, John Herschel Glenn Jr. went to school in New Concord, Ohio, then attended college at Muskingum College, also in New Concord, where he received a degree in engineering. He then followed the aviation traditions of Ohio and enrolled in the Naval Aviation Cadet Program in 1942. Before him were the Wright brothers, who came from Dayton. They created the first airplane capable of short flight. Several Ohioans had been involved at the beginning of the US Air Force during WWI, most notably Lieutenant Frank Patterson, son and nephew of the founder of the National Cash Register Company. He lost his life in a plane crash in 1918. These are the sources of the names for the Wright-Patterson Air Force Base near Dayton, Ohio.

Glenn eventually joined the Marine Fighter Squadron 155 and flew combat missions at the end of World War II. He flew sixty-three missions in Marine Fighter Squadron 311 in the Korean War. By the end of his life, Glenn had put in over nine thousand hours of flight time, three thousand of which were in jets. He was then selected to be part of the new Mercury Space Program, which intended to put an American into space. Glenn was selected to be an astronaut and provided support for Alan Shepard, the first American in space. Glenn piloted the Friendship 7 capsule and became the first American to complete an orbit of Earth. He was hailed as a hero, especially in his home state of Ohio.

Glenn retired from NASA in 1964 and from the Marine Corps in 1965. He had received a seemingly endless list of medals and honors, including the US Astronaut Badge and the Congressional Space Medal of Honor. He became involved in politics and was elected one of Ohio's senators in 1978 and again in 1980, 1986, and 1992; he was the first Ohioan to win four consecutive terms. Then, in 1998, at the age of seventy-seven, he became the oldest astronaut in history when he joined the shuttle *Discovery* in a nine-day mission into orbit to deploy the Spartan solar-observing spacecraft and conduct other experiments. He passed away in Columbus in 2016.

Born just nine years after John Glenn, Neil Armstrong hailed from Wapakoneta, Ohio, a city near the site of a Shawnee village. Armstrong was also a naval aviator and became part of the National Advisory Committee for Aeronautics (NACA). He was stationed at a research center in Cleveland. NACA eventually transformed into the National Aeronautics and Space Administration (NASA). Armstrong became a test pilot and joined the astronaut program in 1962. He was first assigned the command of the Gemini 8 mission and successfully docked two spacecraft for the first time. He was then assigned to lead Apollo 11, which was the mission to go to the moon. As the commander of the mission, Armstrong became the first human being to set foot on the moon in 1969.

Armstrong went on to be a professor at the University of Cincinnati. He served in various capacities as part of commissions on space travel for the federal government and private organizations. He won several awards and honors, including the Congressional Space Medal of Honor, the Explorers Club Medal, and the Congressional Gold Medal. Armstrong passed away in 2012 at the age of eighty-two.

While Glenn and Armstrong were setting records in space, Carl B. Stokes was breaking ground back on Earth. Stokes, born in 1927, became the first black mayor of a major US city when he was elected mayor of Cleveland in 1967. Stokes was born and raised in Cleveland, growing up in Outhwaite, the first federally funded housing project in the city. Stokes served in the US Army and received a bachelor's from the University of Minnesota and a law degree from Cleveland-Marshall Law School. He was admitted to the Ohio Bar in 1957 but eventually went into politics and served in the Ohio House of Representatives. Stokes defeated Seth Taft, grandson of William Howard Taft, for the mayor's seat. He was reelected in 1969.

Stokes helped give city hall jobs to qualified African Americans and women, opening opportunities for more people and fighting discrimination. He chose not to run for a third term and went on to become the first black anchorman in New York City in 1972 but returned to Cleveland in 1980. Stokes went on to serve as a judge until President Bill Clinton appointed him ambassador to the nation of Seychelles. He died of cancer in 1996. In his lifetime, Stokes was honored with fifteen honorary degrees and several awards. The National League of Cities voted him their first black president in 1970.

Also in 1970, Ohio experienced a horrible tragedy that left four dead and a nation stunned when the National Guard opened fire on a crowd of unarmed protesters at what would be known as the Kent State shootings.

On May 4th, 1970, students at Kent State University in Kent, Ohio, gathered to demonstrate against the war in Vietnam. Among the students there that day were Allison Krause and Jeffrey Miller. William Schroeder was watching the protests but not part of them. These three students had no way of knowing this would be their last day on Earth. Another student, Sandra Scheuer, was not part of the demonstration; she was walking to class when she was shot.

The demonstration was a reaction to the seeming escalation of the Vietnam War, which went against President Richard Nixon's previous promise to end the war. The US invaded Cambodia in late April 1970, and the news broke a few days later. Before the demonstration on May 4th, police had been called to the city of Kent to deal with fires, bottles being thrown at cars, and cars being stopped by what seemed to be angry students. Due to the quick escalation, the mayor of Kent asked Governor Jim Rhodes to send the Ohio National Guard.

The National Guard arrived on the campus of Kent State on May 1st. The rally that was held on the 4th was partly anti-war but also opposed the presence of the National Guard on the campus. The authorities at the university felt the rally on the 4th should be prohibited and sent out leaflets explaining the rally was banned. However, three thousand people still showed up for the rally.

The National Guard proceeded to try and disperse the crowd. A jeep circled the protesters, and a bullhorn was used to tell them to leave the common area where they had gathered. This had no effect. Tear gas was shot into the crowd, and the National Guard marched on the rally with loaded rifles. Protesters threw rocks at the guardsmen, but the guardsmen followed students as they left the commons in a haphazard fashion, letting themselves become trapped in a fenced-in football field. Once out of the field, the guardsmen walked up a hill, turned, and fired their weapons. Some shot into the air or ground, but some fired directly into the crowd. Four people were killed. Nine were seriously injured.

Memorial at Kent State, where one of the victim's bodies was found

The guardsmen who fired into the crowd were never determined to have acted unlawfully. Every trial concluded with the belief that the guardsmen had been acting in self-defense. However, many have argued against this interpretation, believing instead that the guardsmen acted out of poor training or even with malicious intent.

The federal and state governments have never held any guardsmen responsible for the students' deaths or injuries, though the state of Ohio settled with the victims and their families for monetary compensation.

The events of May 4th, 1970, might have been much worse if not for the actions of faculty marshals who pleaded with the students for twenty minutes not to retaliate. The shootings provide a clear example of a time when the US was divided and is a stark lesson on what happens when those divisions become too great and spill over into violence.

On January 26th, 1978, a very different type of problem fell over the state in the form of a devastating blizzard. Cold winds came from the west, reaching seventy and even eighty miles an hour in some cases. Temperatures fell by thirty degrees in about two hours. Snowfall was estimated to be about fifteen inches, and the high winds created snow drifts that reached above one-story buildings. Rail and highway travel was stopped, as was air travel. Businesses and schools closed for several days; things did not return to normal for at least a week. Interstate 75, which runs through the middle of the state, was closed for three days. Several people were isolated; some were stranded on highways and broke into truck weigh stations for shelter.

As the temperature fell to $0°$ Fahrenheit, Lake Erie began to ice over, and ships became stranded. Utility poles were knocked over in the wind, knocking out telephone and electricity to several communities. Food shortages became a concern, and in some cases, National Guard helicopters were used to deliver food to stranded citizens.

Thankfully, the storm came in the early morning on a Thursday, so no children were stranded in buses or in schools due to the storm. A total of fifty-one people lost their lives in the blizzard, mostly from exposure when they left a broken-down car or from being in a building that collapsed under the weight of a snow drift. On a positive note, there were no traffic accident fatalities that weekend because almost every highway and road were closed. The blizzard was still a tragedy. Less than ten years later, another tragedy would hit Ohio in a completely different way.

Following in the footsteps of John Glenn and Neil Armstrong, Judith Resnik applied to NASA in 1977. She was one of six women accepted into the program. Resnik was born in Akron to first-generation Jewish-Russian immigrant parents. She attended Carnegie Tech (now called Carnegie Mellon) in Pittsburgh, Pennsylvania, and earned a degree in electrical engineering. In 1971, she earned a master's degree from the University of Maryland. She became the second American woman to go to space in 1984 when she was chosen to be part of the crew for the shuttle *Discovery*. As part of this mission, she unfurled the 102-foot-long solar sail that would be used in later missions to harness the sun's energy. Resnik was set to go back to space on the shuttle *Challenger* in 1986. Seventy-three seconds into the flight, *Challenger* exploded due to a failed seal because of the cold, killing everyone on board. It was a tragic end for such a promising astronaut. Closer to home, politics in Ohio at the end of the twentieth century would prove to be not unlike politics in any other period.

In 1982, Richard Celeste of Cleveland was elected governor of Ohio; he was a Democrat. He had previously been the director of the Peace Corps under President Jimmy Carter and had studied at Yale and Oxford in England as a Rhodes Scholar. Celeste raised income tax rates to combat an ongoing recession. The tax rate was unpopular but allowed him to improve various areas like education and mental health systems. Despite some scandal, Celeste was elected for a second term. He established a cabinet-level agency to deal with illicit drugs and alcohol addiction recovery. He left office in 1991 and later became an ambassador to India.

For most of the 1990s, Ohio's governor was Republican George Voinovich. Voinovich was born in Cleveland and was mayor of that city for much of the 1980s. As mayor, he saw Cleveland rebound from a serious financial crisis. As governor, he eliminated the General Assistance welfare program and put through $1 billion in tax increases to battle a climbing deficit.

Voinovich's two terms were a bit of a mixed bag. He helped to keep spending down and increased support for preschool programs, but his former chief of staff was sentenced to six months in prison for a severe ethics violation. Voinovich went on to take John Glenn's seat as a US senator in 1998.

Nancy Putnam Hollister became Ohio's first woman governor in 1998. She had previously been mayor of Marietta. She was, in fact, related to General Rufus Putnam, who had helped found Marietta and begin the settling of Ohio. Hollister went to Kent State University and married attorney Jeff Hollister in 1970. She was the first woman elected as lieutenant governor of Ohio and became governor when Governor Voinovich stepped down to become a US senator. Hollister was only governor for eleven days before she was succeeded by Robert Taft, great-grandson of William Howard Taft.

For the later part of the 20th century, the Democrats retained most of the political power in Ohio, despite the fact that a Republican, James A. Rhodes, was governor for much of the 1970s. The 1980s were dominated by Governor Celeste and his highly effective Democrat machine. However, things began to change in the 1990s, thanks partly to questions being raised about the morality of Celeste's machine. This led to Voinovich and the Republicans sweeping the elections in the 1990s. In Voinovich's second run for governor, he won almost 72 percent of the vote.

However, Republicans now faced the same questions that had plagued Democrats in the previous decade. Questions centered almost exclusively around campaign finances. Voinovich put through campaign finance reforms that provided limits to contributions, but several loopholes existed that allowed people to give loans or in-kind donations of any amount. The loans would often be forgiven without politicians paying anything back, thereby creating unlimited potential for contributions. State Treasurer Joseph T. Deters received $50,000 from a Cleveland investment broker, though this was well beyond the stipulated limits. He had a loophole to thank for such a generous contribution.

The 1990s also offered an interesting, though perhaps puzzling, distraction when the city of Columbus wanted to mark the five-hundredth anniversary of Christopher Columbus's first voyage to the "New World." They eventually settled on AmeriFlora '92, a vast horticultural exhibit in Franklin Park that was open from April to October 1992. There seems to be no obvious connection between Christopher Columbus, after whom the city is named, and a display of flowers and plants, but this didn't stop the city from bringing the two ideas together. The inspiration for a floral show seems to have been large-scale displays in Spain, France, and Montreal.

One thing that planners failed to take notice of was the concerns of people living near Franklin Park, a predominantly black community. These residents pointed out they used Franklin Park but had no voice in the decision to build the floral exhibit, which closed down the park for almost the entire year.

The show encompassed over 160 acres and was expected to bring in 5 million visitors. The show featured an exhibit by the Smithsonian called "Seeds of Change" that discussed corn, potatoes, sugar, horses, and disease. A Community of Nations featured gardens that represented Japan, India, Russia, and Monaco, among others. Another exhibit displayed common elements of American backyard gardens, and there was a showcase of Disney topiaries, which were living sculptures of Mickey, Mary Poppins, and Roger Rabbit.

President George Bush, First Lady Barbara Bush, Governor Voinovich, and Bob Hope were part of the grand opening. While it proved a boost to Columbus businesses, the attendance was almost three million short of what was anticipated. It was reportedly a financial loss, but once it was over, many residents appreciated the improvements that were brought to Franklin Park as a result.

In 1970, Ohio's total population reached over ten million for the first time. It increased by 100,000 in the 1980s and 1990s. In 1980, the African American population reached 10 percent of the total population for the first time, having a population of over a million. By the end of the 20th century, Ohio had clearly become a largely urban state, with 75 percent of the population living in the cities while only 25 percent lived in what was considered rural.

In 1976, Katherine Crumbly became Ohio's first female sheriff in Belmont County. Toledo elected its first woman mayor, Donna Owens, in 1983. November 8th, 1994, saw the election of Nancy Putman Hollister as the first woman lieutenant governor, Betty D. Montgomery as the first woman elected as attorney general, and John Kenneth Blackwell as the first African American elected state treasurer. To date, Ohio has never had an African American governor nor a woman elected to the position.

The 1980s and 1990s saw a population shift in Ohio. Once densely populated city centers began to lose residents, outlying regions around the cities grew rapidly. It was the rise of the suburbs in the Buckeye State. Cities in Ohio had long had suburban areas, especially once the automobile was adopted. However, city centers remained largely populated throughout the 20th century until the phenomenon that became known as "urban sprawl."

Some of this was racially motivated. Some whites living in cities saw the increasing black population as a threat because of the racist views they held; due to their beliefs, they commenced what was called the "white flight" out of cities and into suburban areas. Many people just wanted to get out of the congested city areas, desiring to have larger plots of land that were often cheaper outside a city's limits. However, those who moved to the suburbs often found the populations there rising. Over the course of several years, suburbs took on many of the urban problems that people had originally sought to escape.

At the same time, cities continually annexed various neighborhoods, so footprints for cities like Cincinnati, Cleveland, and Columbus grew substantially. The area of Columbus, in particular, grew fivefold from 1950 to 2000. In 1990, Columbus became the largest city in Ohio, surpassing Cleveland. In 1970, Cleveland was the tenth-largest American city by population. In 1980, no Ohio cities were in the top ten; Cleveland was eighteenth, Columbus was nineteenth, Cincinnati was thirty-second, and Toledo was fortieth. In 1990, Columbus was sixteenth, Cleveland had fallen to twenty-third, Cincinnati was forty-second, while Toledo was forty-ninth.

On November 7th, 1994, tragedy struck Wickliffe Middle School in Wickliffe, Ohio. An apparently mentally troubled former student named Keith Ledeger walked into the school with a loaded shotgun. In less than four minutes, he fired ten shots, wounding three people and killing custodian Peter Christopher before he was shot and subdued by a Wickliffe police officer. This was at a time when school shootings were unheard of; it was before the Columbine High School shooting of 1999. The community was shocked. No active shooter plans or emergency response drills were in place for situations like this because it was simply unthinkable. The school had been unlocked. Anyone could have walked in. Ledeger's motive was never fully obtained, and he died in prison.

Chapter 10 – The Recent Past and Future

The dawn of the 21st century revealed Ohio was a state of contradictions. Politically, the northeast remained heavily Democrat, the southwest was mainly Republican, while the center of the state often contained independent swing voters. Cities that had once been among the largest in the country were now past their glory days. Industries still flourished, but the new global market meant many manufacturing jobs were now done overseas. A deep system of history still held the state together. The year 2003 marked the bicentennial of statehood, as it had been two hundred years since the first General Assembly had met to decide the future of the state called Ohio.

Robert A. Taft III was governor from 1999 to 2007. The great-grandson of a president, grandson of a US senator, and son of another US senator, Taft seemed destined to be an important political figure. He had a degree from Yale and another from Princeton and joined the Peace Corps, where he taught school in East Africa. Taft served as the Hamilton County commissioner, state representative, and secretary of the state of Ohio before winning the governorship.

Taft was a Republican but called for spending increases once he took power. He was especially instrumental in getting public schools refurbished. In 2003, he signed a $48.8 billion budget that included large tax increases. The state sales tax was raised from 5 percent to 6 percent during Taft's second term. However, the state was losing jobs, and the economy was suffering, so he cut income taxes for five years and reduced the sales tax to 5.5 percent. Taft also began the Third Frontier project, which sought to encourage technological jobs and research in the state.

Taft's tenure was not without scandal. The state's Workers' Compensation department was found to have awarded about $50 million to a Republican fundraiser; the Republican used millions for his personal use. In 2005, Taft was found guilty of four ethics misdemeanors in Franklin County Municipal Court. With that conviction, Taft became the first sitting governor to be convicted of a crime. Taft left the governor's office in 2007 and took a position at the University of Dayton.

From 2007 to 2011, Ted Strickland was governor. Strickland was a Methodist minister with humble origins. Strickland, an Appalachian Democrat, beat J. Kenneth Blackwell in the general election. Strickland signed legislation to ensure that 75 percent of Ohio's electricity came from renewable sources by 2025. He froze tuition at all state universities. He also supported the Third Frontier project. Strickland reversed his stance on gambling by allowing slot machines at racetracks. This eventually led to four sanctioned casinos opening in the state.

Under Strickland, Ohio fell into a great recession, as it saw a significant loss in jobs. Unemployment stayed at around 11 percent. Thanks in large part to these issues, Strickland lost his attempt at a second term to Republican John Kasich.

John R. Kasich ran on a promise to bring jobs to Ohio. He had previously been a US representative and had led the budget committee. Kasich had considered running for president in 1999 but stepped aside and supported George W. Bush. He was known for having worked with Democrats to find wasteful government spending and identify corporate tax loopholes. Kasich left his role as a representative and became a managing director for Lehman Brothers, an investment firm, and a commentator for FOX News.

With the economy in a recession, Kasich felt obliged to run for the governor's seat and won in a contested battle with Ted Strickland. Lehman Brothers had collapsed in the recession, but this had no effect on Kasich's approval.

Kasich immediately set about balancing the state's budget. He slashed aid to schools and local governments. He sold five state prisons to private companies and leased the state's wholesale liquor monopoly to a private company called JobsOhio. He fought against unions and hoped to take away bargaining rights, which were rejected by the voters.

In his second term, Kasich expanded Medicaid coverage, which upset many of his supporters. He went on to run for the Republican nomination for president in 2016 but lost to Donald Trump. Kasich never gave Trump his support and openly opposed Trump while he was president. He spoke at the Democratic National Convention in 2020 to show support for Joe Biden.

In 2000, the Big Pig Gig took place in Cincinnati and saw the installation of public art that featured decorated fiber-glass pigs in reference to Cincinnati's past as "Porkopolis." These pigs were placed around the city in prominent locations and at popular businesses.

In 2001, the streets of Cincinnati were much less whimsical when a series of street riots broke out. These riots stemmed from demonstrations over the perceived poor response to the police shooting of an unarmed African American youth named Timothy Thomas. A city-wide curfew was enacted, similar to the Cincinnati Courthouse riots of 1884. The curfew allowed emotions to settle, and peace returned to the streets.

A series of shootings around Interstate 270 near Columbus caused widespread panic in 2003. One person, Gail Knisley, was killed. The shooter shot at traffic, homes, and a school building. It was determined to be a sniper shooting, with the suspect using a high-powered rifle. Eventually, a suspect, Charles A. McCoy Jr., was caught in Las Vegas. He pled guilty to the shootings and received twenty-seven years in prison.

Also, in Columbus, a nightclub shooting happened in 2004 in which four people were murdered and three others injured. The shooter, Nathan Gale, was apparently targeting "Dimebag" Darrell Abbott, who was performing with his band Damage Plan at the club. Gale was shot and killed at the scene by a police officer. His motive for shooting and killing Abbott remains largely unknown.

On a much lighter note, Ohio was the shooting location for many famous films. *The Shawshank Redemption* (1994) was set in Maine but was filmed largely in the Sandusky area. *Rain Man* (1988) was filmed largely in Cincinnati. Cleveland was the location for the filming of *A Christmas Story* (1983). Cleveland also supplied the backdrop for superhero flicks, such as *The Avengers* (2012) and *Captain America: The Winter Soldier* (2014). Sandusky was the fictional and actual setting for much of *Tommy Boy* (1995).

Part of Ohio's history, especially in more recent years, has been a story of preservation. Thousands of years ago, the land was home to many different people and societies. Ohioans have been increasingly interested in keeping that history alive by preserving and restoring historically important places and memorializing important people and events through monuments. For instance, there are seventy-six National Historic Landmarks within the state. Some of these are ancient, like the aptly named Fort Ancient, an earthwork complex built by Native Americans who lived in the area from 200 BCE to 400 CE. There are also earthwork sites from the Hopewell culture at Hopeton Earthworks and Newark Earthworks. Most notable perhaps is Serpent Mound, a massive earthwork built by the Fort Ancient culture in the shape of a giant serpent. This site most likely had great spiritual significance to Native Americans who called Ohio home.

There are also several sites connected to the US presidents who called Ohio home. There is the James A. Garfield home in Mentor, the Ulysses S. Grant Boyhood Home in Georgetown, the Warren G. Harding home in Marion, the William McKinley National Memorial in Canton, the Alphonso Taft home in Cincinnati (birthplace of William Howard Taft), and Spiegel Grove, which was the home of Rutherford B. Hayes.

The Wright Flyer III is a 1905 plane built by the Wright brothers and can be seen in their hometown of Dayton, as well as the Wright Cycling Company and Print Shop. Another part of the Wright story and aviation history can be found at Huffman Prairie in Fairborn, a large field where the Wright Brothers tested their early aircraft and trained themselves to be the first pilots in history. In Oakwood, one can find Hawthorn Hill, the mansion Orville Wright built in 1914.

Houses are not the only historically important sites that have been preserved in Ohio. In Cincinnati, there is the stunning Music Hall, the Observatory, and Union Terminal, the latter of which was originally a luxurious train station in the West Side neighborhood but is now home to the Cincinnati Museum Center. The Cleveland Arcade, built in 1890, features two nine-story towers connected by a five-story arcade with a glass roof. It was partially financed by John D. Rockefeller. The Covington and Cincinnati Suspension Bridge, otherwise known as the Roebling Bridge, was one of the first of its kind and became a prototype for the Brooklyn Bridge, which was also built by the Roebling Company. The Fallen Timbers Battlefield in Maumee is another historic landmark of great significance to the history of Ohio, as is the site of Fort Meigs in Perrysburg.

Off the coast of Sandusky, in Lake Erie, is Johnson's Island, which was home to a large prisoner of war camp during the American Civil War. More than fifteen thousand Confederate soldiers, spies, guerilla soldiers, and political prisoners called it home during the war, and the island is now a National Historic Landmark. There are also some towboats, a showboat, and one submarine that have been preserved for history in the rivers and lakes of Ohio, as well as a section of the Miami and Erie Canal, which had once been a tremendously important artery for the state.

The idea of preserving Ohio's history is not a new one, of course. The Ohio Historical Society was founded in 1885 but is now called Ohio History Connection. It maintains over fifty historical sites and museums. Over the past ten years, it has seen steady growth despite economic hardships. This demonstrates Ohio's and Ohioans' commitment to preserving their colorful history to share it with residents and future generations. According to Ohio History Connection's most recently available yearly report, they have approximately 233,000 visitors to their sites and museums per year and gave $130,900 in grant money to organizations throughout the state in 2021. The visitor numbers are most likely below normal totals due to the recent pandemic, which has taken a toll on many non-profit organizations in the past few years.

As Ohio now comes upon its 220th anniversary, the people remain committed to a prosperous future while retaining their celebrated past. The state has achieved quite a lot, and with the introduction of new industries and the continued determination of the people that call it home, Ohio seems poised to achieve even more in the centuries ahead. While it remains a land of contradictions and constant change, it also retains the pioneering spirit and strong work ethic that has made it such an important state.

Conclusion

The first human beings to live in the land that would be called Ohio are relatively unknown. Archaeologists know they were there, especially from the distinctive spear points they left behind, but they don't know much about their society or culture. They are often called Paleo-Indians, a catch-all term that belies the reality that they were here tens of thousands of years ago. Then came the so-called "mound builders," another catch-all term for Native American societies that constructed earthworks for burials, ceremonial purposes, and perhaps as a means of defense. Archaeologists and historians do not know what these people called themselves, but they have been given names reflecting the sites of these earthworks. There is Fort Ancient, Hopewell, and Adena, to name a few. These people seemed to have existed alongside and sometimes were part of the Mississippian culture that also built mounds farther to the west. Archaeologists have retrieved pottery, pipes, figurines, and jewelry made of materials like seashells, copper, and precious stones from some of the burial mounds. These items show the cultures of Ohio traded with cultures out west, along the East Coast, and as far south as what is today Mexico. Eventually, war and disease changed the makeup of these groups in large part due to the arrival of the Spanish, Dutch, English, and French fisherman, settlers, and traders over the course of hundreds of years.

The Native Americans moved west from the eastern coast of what would be the US and settled among the remains of the mound-building cultures in Ohio. The Americans who began to settle the Northwest Territory saw discovered that many of the tribes were amalgamations of people who had previously been part of separate cultures. These tribes blended their languages, rituals, religions, and ideas. Tribes like the Shawnee recognized that places like Serpent Mound were important and held rituals there that coincided with the spring and fall equinox, but they could not tell the early American explorers who had built the mounds, as the details had been lost.

At first, the Americans appreciated the mounds and other important Native American sites, but eventually, progress quite literally bulldozed over them. It was not until fairly recently that American archaeologists and historians began to take a closer look at these sites and paid more attention to the Native Americans' stories about these places and the people who built them. Serpent Mound, for instance, had many mysteries surrounding it: who had built it, when, and for what reason? Recent work by Ohio History Connection makes a strong argument that the people of the Fort Ancient culture built it almost a thousand years ago and that it represents a creation story involving the Great Serpent and the First Woman. The part of the mound that most likely represented the First Woman was unknowingly leveled and is now part of the path that encircles the mound today.

That is a lot of background information for a conclusion, but the point is that the history of Ohio is being rewritten even today. Things that were unknown or once thought are now being clarified or questioned. The history of Ohio, much like the history of any place where people have lived and died, is ongoing and ever-changing. It is a living creature in and of itself and cannot be expected to sit still for any amount of time. As we look back at the long story of Ohio, from ancient mounds to American settlers, from the wars between Americans and Native Americans to America's war against itself, from the presidents, astronauts, freedom fighters, and titans of industry to the schools, art, tragedies, and politics, Ohio shows itself as a patchwork of humanity that speaks to the rest of the American Midwest and to the United States as a whole. The people there always strive for excellence, however that person might define that term.

The history of Ohio is a complicated history, and this book only attempts to highlight the most important moments and people who helped shape it and who represented Ohio to the rest of the world. Many places and people seem incredibly intertwined. One cannot imagine Marietta without Rufus Putnam or Cleveland without John D. Rockefeller.

Largely because of its geography, Ohio has long been a place of industry, but it has also been home to industrious people. The council of Akron had the foresight to attract BF Goodrich to their city, thus beginning a great rubber manufacturing kingdom. Procter & Gamble has helped maintain a monolith of consumer products that stretches around the globe, and all of it started as a humble soap- and candle-making business in Cincinnati. Cleveland's oil refineries were the largest in the nation for many years and helped to make Cleveland the famous city it is today.

From the bus driver to the CEO to the waiter, Ohioans are city people, but perhaps paradoxically, much of the state is wide-open farm fields. A drive across the state will be primarily remembered as bucolic scenes of rolling pastures and corn fields with the occasional intrusion of a large city. There are people in those farmhouses and along the winding roads in the Appalachian foothills whose lives are not entirely unlike the lives of the people who lived there a hundred years ago. Of course, today, almost everyone enjoys a Wi-Fi connection and has their smartphone in hand.

One might wonder what a Paleo-Indian, a Shawnee of 1812, a conductor on the Underground Railroad, a factory worker from Columbus in the early 20th century, a college student from the 1980s, and someone from today might say to each other if they were magically able to understand one another. Of course, there might be marvels at new technology and questions concerning the outcomes of wars, economic panics, and international politics, but at the end of the day, it seems most likely that it would be hospitable conversations about friends, family, and their homeland of Ohio. The land will remain long after the people are gone, and it remembers the stories that occur on it. It will speak to anyone who cares to listen to the long and interesting story of a place called Ohio.

Part 2: Ulysses S. Grant

A Captivating Guide to the American General Who Served as the 18th President of the United States of America

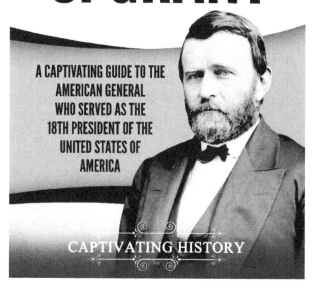

Introduction

- He Was a General, a Gentleman, and a Scholar—and He Also Happened to be the 18th President

People in the United States see his face staring up at them from the $50 bill. Printed on this pale green material, Grant looks stoic, if not a bit uncomfortable. In fact, a bit of aloofness and a chronic sense of restlessness was a permanent feature of this former president and general.

Ulysses S. Grant is often remembered in heroic terms. And rightly enough. He was a man whose courage managed to command respect even from his enemies, both on the battlefield and in the political arena. Even so, as with many legendary figures, layers of embellishment built up over the years that cover the real man.

Grant certainly was not perfect. He tended to be overly sensitive and had bouts of melancholy at times. An acute episode of depression actually led Grant to drop out of the military as a young man. It would take several years of hardship and the eruption of the Civil War to get Grant reinstated.

Grant's temperament could indeed be unpredictable at times, but the great thing about Ulysses S. Grant was his determination. Once there was a task at hand, he knew he would complete it. Grant knew, for example, that the North would ultimately win the Civil War. He knew that it was just a matter of national endurance to see the war through to the end.

Grant was ultimately a man of action; he could not stand the feeling of listless idleness. He did not mind putting out fires, and he happily moved from one complex issue to the next. On the contrary, it was sitting and waiting with nothing to do that Grant disliked. It was perhaps for this reason that this two-term president came to dislike the presidency so much in his later years.

For Grant, the presidency was far too ephemeral for his tastes. He knew that much of his work in politics could be easily undone by others. After realizing the transitory nature of the presidency, he would ultimately decline what would have been a third term. Nevertheless, he has gone down as a man of the ages. Here is the story of that stoic figure on the $50 bill—here is the story of Ulysses S. Grant.

Chapter 1 – From Georgetown to West Point

"Nations, like individuals, are punished for their transgressions."

-Ulysses S. Grant

Ulysses S. Grant was a product of what was at that time the still rugged frontier country of Ohio. He was the son of a man by the name of Jesse Root Grant. The elder Grant was known as a no-nonsense craftsman who worked with his hands and led with his heart. He was a tanner by trade, producing leather goods such as shoes and saddles. As an ambitious and driven young man, Jesse caught the attention of one Hannah Simpson.

After a whirlwind courtship, the couple married, and it was from this union that Ulysses S. Grant was born on April 27th, 1822. Grant's full name at birth was actually Hiram Ulysses Grant. His family tended to simply call him Ulysses and sometimes even by the shortened variation of "Lyss." In later years, Grant would drop Hiram altogether and just go by Ulysses. Many might wonder then where the "S" in Ulysses S. Grant comes from? That was actually the product of a typo.

We are getting a bit ahead of the chronological narrative of Grant's life, but in order to avoid confusion, this story is worth telling at the beginning. The incident occurred when Ulysses was seeking admittance to West Point. He received a recommendation from an Ohio congressman by the name of Thomas Hamer. It was Hamer who accidentally printed Ulysses's full name as being "Ulysses S. Grant."

In reality, there is no "S" in Ulysses's name, so therefore the "S" does not stand for anything at all. After his successful acceptance at West Point, Ulysses discovered that the name "Ulysses S. Grant" had stuck, and he just went with it for the rest of his life. Now with that little aside out of the way, let us take a look at the early days of the man we have come to know as Ulysses S. Grant.

He was the oldest child in his family, although many siblings would follow him. His brother Samuel was born in 1825, and he had a sister Clara in 1828. Another sister named Virginia popped up in 1832, then a brother named Orvil in 1835, and finally one more little sister by the name of Mary in 1839. Ulysses and his brothers and sisters grew up in the cozy confines of Georgetown, Ohio.

Grant first attended school at the age of five. It was one of those classic one-room schoolhouses that became so ubiquitous on the frontier. It may have had its rustic charms, but his lessons certainly were not free. His parents dutifully paid the yearly fee so that their children could go to school. The school lessons, as one might expect in those days, consisted of basic reading, writing, and arithmetic.

It was nothing too in-depth, just the basics of knowing how to read, sign one's name, and add and subtract. It was the latter that the young Ulysses seemed to excel. His quick mind always outdid his peers when it came to shouting out the answers to math problems. Even so, his school year was very short in duration, purportedly only stretching throughout the winter months. Ulysses would be back at home helping his parents with various household chores as soon as spring arrived.

Back on the old homestead, Grant, like many other children of his time and place, became proficient with firearms. However, the interesting thing about Grant was the fact that while other young men developed their abilities with the rifle, Grant was always keen to practice his luck with a handgun. Since hunting—the primary goal of becoming a good shot in the backwoods—was not done with handguns, this was a bit unusual. But nevertheless, Grant became a good marksman.

Along with his education and ability as a skilled marksman, Grant was an avid lover of horses and had developed a finely honed level of horsemanship. It has been said that Grant rode horses ever since he was a little boy. Ulysses was especially good at calming wild and unruly horses, which is a great skill to have in an age when so much depended upon horse travel. His abilities can be demonstrated from one tale of his youth. It was said that he had a new untamed horse leading him in a buggy when the steed suddenly decided to bolt.

The horse was unresponsive to the reins, and it took Grant on a wild ride across the countryside. As the story goes, the horse nearly led Grant off the edge of a steep cliff. The animal managed to stop, and the quick-thinking Ulysses had an idea. He took a bandana and wrapped it around the maddened horse's eyes. As strange as this might sound, the darkness of not being able to see calmed the spooked horse. Grant was able to lead the now blinded animal back home merely by his own direction on the reins.

It is said that Ulysses purchased his first horse at the age of nine. He had worked part-time hauling wood, and he was ready to use his earnings to get a horse of his own. The story in itself provides us with an amusing anecdote of a young man eager to buy a horse. However, he was not well-versed in negotiating.

His father had apparently tried to haggle with the seller on the price, offering $20, but the seller refused. Ulysses's father instructed his son to go to the seller and try to offer $20 himself to see what the seller might do. His dad advised him that if the seller again refused to then offer $22.50. If he refused this amount, then Ulysses should tell him that he was willing to pay as much as $25. This is pretty sound advice for negotiating a business deal, but the naïve Ulysses ended up showing his cards.

The seller point-blank asked him, "How much did your father tell you to pay?" To which Ulysses steadfastly replied, "Papa says I may offer you $20 for the colt, but if you won't take that, I am to offer $22.50. And if you won't take that, to give you $25." With perhaps a chuckle or two of surprise, the wily seller cut the negotiations short by informing the young man that he could not possibly accept anything less than $25.

Ulysses got his horse, but the details of the deal were passed around to other locals, and soon his peers were laughing at his expense. Ulysses was likened to being a simpleton, and they began to tease Grant by calling him "Useless" Grant. This ridicule deeply affected Grant, and he would have a tendency to be quite sensitive to any form of mockery leveled at him in the future.

As he grew older, Grant expressed his dislike of working at his father's tannery. It was a laborious, often gruesome business, after all, which involved soaking animal skins in lime. And the tedious work of plucking out hair certainly was not pleasant. His abilities with horses won him a way out, as Grant would be the one responsible for loading up his saddle with his father's latest goods and taking them to market.

He would also equip his horses with a buggy and chauffeur people back and forth, offering rides to paying customers and taking them as far away as Chillicothe, Ohio, which was some sixty miles away. These travels when he was just a young man would give Ulysses a sense of the larger world around him. Many believe that it was his days as a horse chauffer that instilled in him a desire to see lands far removed from his familiar family homestead.

Jesse, by all accounts, was proud of his son. When Ulysses was a young boy, Jesse would profess that his eldest child was destined for great things. And according to one tantalizing anecdote, Jesse was not the only one. It has been said that on one occasion, a visiting phrenologist declared as much as well.

Phrenologists were infamous in the 19th century for supposedly gleaning the standout characteristics of people through their physical features. They were sort of like the 19th-century version of a fortune teller and chiropractor combined. Phrenologists felt around on people's heads, necks, and shoulders to try and decipher what a person was like.

This particular phrenologist is said to have studied the young Ulysses intently. After taking a look at his head shape, he came away absolutely delighted. The phrenologist solemnly proclaimed, "It is no very common head! It is an extraordinary head!"

As Jesse and his son stared in wonder, the man then added, "It would not be strange if we should see him President of the United States!" Most today would probably assume this man was just out to make a quick buck from a parent like Jesse who was eager to pay to hear such good news. There likely was nothing "extraordinary" about Grant's head, especially since phrenology has been deemed a pseudoscience today. But perhaps his words planted a seed in Ulysses's mind. As most of us know, Ulysses S. Grant was indeed destined to become a US president.

Shortly after the phrenologist's proclamation, in 1836, the budding Ulysses Grant, then fourteen years old, was delivered to Maysville, Kentucky, to attend seminary school. Here, he found himself somewhat disenchanted with the curriculum, which did not seem much more challenging than what he had learned in the single-room schoolhouse back home. He did manage to get involved with a debate team, which allowed him to stimulate his mind. He debated the important topics of the day, such as ending slavery and whether or not the newly independent territory of Texas should be admitted to the Union.

Ulysses Grant would return home to Georgetown by the time spring had arrived. He would reach a turning point in his young life when he finally let his father know that he did not intend to follow him into the tanning business. This frank discussion occurred in the summer of 1838 after Ulysses was forced to help his father out with his work. Ulysses was made to stretch hides over beams and scrape hair from the skins.

In the midst of this work, which Ulysses found incredibly distasteful, he told his father that his mind was made up. He remarked to his dear old dad, "Father, this tanning is not the kind of work I like. I'll work at it, though, if you wish me to, until I am twenty-one. But you may depend on it, I'll never work a day at it after that." His father was surprisingly lenient with Ulysses, considering the harshness of the time in which parents were often strict enforcers of their will.

His dad is said to have told his son, "I want you to work at whatever you like and intend to follow. Now, what do you think you like?" Ulysses admitted that there were three paths he was thinking about taking. He explained to his father that he could see himself either being a trader, a farmer, or simply going on to further his education by attending college.

Farming was a noble enterprise, and it was one that Grant respected. However, it would have made the young man stationary. He did not desire to stay in one place, so he considered becoming a trader, making a living trading goods on a riverboat going up and down the Mississippi. It would have been a profitable enough enterprise, but traders tended to be unstable socially. Many of them had a penchant for drinking, gambling, and womanizing. Ulysses knew his parents would not enjoy such a prospect.

His parents were staunch Methodists, but they were surprisingly lenient with their son when it came to church. He was never forced to go to church on Sunday if he did not want to, and Grant would largely remain agnostic for much of his life.

And he was not only agnostic with religion in those days; he was also agnostic with politics.

In today's polarizing times, in which almost everyone seems to take one side or the other, it may be hard for us to imagine. However, as a young man, Grant did not have any real political leanings. He just lived his life and left politics to others. Interestingly enough, although Grant, who is often viewed as the true successor of Abraham Lincoln, would one day become a Republican president, it was a Democrat who paved the way for the furtherance of Grant's education.

In 1839, a seventeen-year-old Grant sought to enroll at West Point to become an officer. His father Jesse had lobbied a Democrat congressman by the name of Thomas L. Hamer for aid in securing Grant's enrollment. Hamer represented the Grant family's district in Ohio. Jesse contacted the congressman and saw to it that he recommended his son for enrollment at West Point.

Jesse was the one who came up with the whole idea, thinking that West Point would give Grant the higher education he desired. And if he was accepted, the US government would even foot the bill. The ploy worked. After Grant passed the entrance exam, he was duly enrolled that fall. As mentioned above, the helpful Congressman Hamer accidentally referred to the new young cadet as "Ulysses S. Grant" in his entrance papers—thereby branding him for life with a meaningless middle initial.

Grant had to remain at a boarding facility filled with West Point applicants for two weeks before he received word that he had passed the test. Once cleared, he was then off to get a haircut and get fitted for a uniform. Here, Grant was utterly amazed at the work of Joe the barber, who was able to cut down a new recruit's hair to virtually nothing all with just a pair of scissors. These were the days before electronic clippers, so the fact that this man was able to cut their hair down to just stubble atop their head must have truly been impressive.

After that, these clean-cut recruits headed off to the barracks of West Point. Upon their arrival, the greatest hurdle they faced was the older students, who mercilessly teased these new recruits as soon as they saw them. Another humiliation was the fact that it was a custom to teach the new cadets how to dance. The idea of teaching soldiers ballroom dancing might seem a bit ridiculous today, and the fact that the school forced these awkward young men to dance together made it all the more absurd.

Nevertheless, on September 14th, 1839, Grant made his commitments clear. He signed his official documents of enlistment, with the words, "I, Cadet U.S. Grant do hereby engage, with the consent of my guardian, to serve in the Army of the United States for eight years, unless sooner discharged by the proper authority." It was with these solemn words that Grant had committed himself to the austere life of the West Point Barracks.

His days would begin early, at around five in the morning. He would be woken up to the sound of the military drum roll, which served as an alarm clock. Ulysses Grant is said to have developed a distaste for loud music. Many believe that it likely stems from these rude awakenings, with this blaring martial, military music. The drum beats woke him up and then accompanied him to class, and he heard them once again before he went to sleep at night.

Nevertheless, Grant was determined to make it—drumming and all. And he was not only going to make it; he was going to grow to like it. This was evidenced by a letter he wrote back home to a cousin of his shortly into his stay. In it, he had suddenly become surprisingly upbeat. The young cadet penned, "West point is decidedly the most beautiful place I have ever seen. From the window near by [sic] I can see the Hudson...Its bosom studded with hundreds of snow white sails...On the whole I would not go away on any account. The fact is if a man graduates here he is safer fer [sic] life. Let him go where he will. There is much to dislike but more to like. I mean to study hard and stay if possible. Contrary to you and the rest of my friends I have not been the least homesick—no!"

He was a fairly popular cadet by the recollection of most who knew him. And those who did would recall that the young man was often called "Uncle Sam" or sometimes just "Sam" due to his first two initials being "U. S." But not everyone was always so kind to Grant.

In one instance, which historians have often retold, he was severely tested by a bigger cadet who decided to try his luck bullying Grant. According to the story, Grant was simply in line at the mess hall, waiting to get his food just like everyone else, when fellow cadet Jack Lindsay suddenly shoved him out of the line, as if he were going to take his place.

Grant, who was used to talking his way out of problems back home, was surprisingly patient with the uncouth youth, telling him to simply be more careful in the future. But when Lindsay tried to shove Grant again, all hell broke loose. An animalistic rage erupted from Grant, and he leaped upon his tormenter, knocking him to the ground.

Grant then began pummeling his foe with his hammer-like mitts. His hands were indeed iron-strong from his many years of helping his dad tan hides, as well as his many hours controlling wild horses. As such, Grant, even though he was smaller than this blowhard bully, was able to make short work of him. Lindsay was beaten so badly that from that day forward, no one messed with Ulysses S. Grant. He would be allowed to eat in the mess hall in peace.

Chapter 2 – Graduation and the First Call of Duty

"There never was a time when, in my opinion, some way could not be found to prevent the drawing of the sword."

-Ulysses S. Grant

After two years at West Point, Grant was given the customary sixty-day leave that was given to second-year students. He took this time to head home to his folks in Ohio. His family had since moved to the town of Bethel, which was about ten miles away from Georgetown.

In May of 1841, this young cadet was seen getting off a stagecoach near Bethel and then paying a local driver to transport him the rest of his journey by horse-drawn buggy. Upon dropping off this elegantly clad young man in his crisp West Point uniform, the driver figured his family would come rushing out to greet him. This was not the case.

Ulysses S. Grant was known later in life as being a fairly reserved fellow, and his family was of a similar disposition. Instead of rushing out to say how much they missed him and how glad they were to see him, his family delivered characteristic flatline responses. His mother and father simply asked, "How are you, son?" And likewise, his younger siblings simply inquired, "How are you, brother?"

At any rate, after this slight reprieve with his folks, Grant was back at West Point to finish the rest of his tenure at the school. Upon his return, he was promoted to the rank of sergeant in the Corps of Cadets. His greatest challenge in finishing up what remained of his coursework was math. Grant had been quite good at general mathematics during his elementary education back in Ohio, but he found higher mathematics, such as algebra, more challenging.

Nevertheless, he not only cracked the secret to succeeding in algebra but also excelled in geometry, trigonometry, and calculus. With higher math conquered, there was nothing left to hold this cadet back.

At West Point, Grant also carried on his passion for horse riding, and he became known as a proficient horseman by his peers. This was important since being able to serve as an officer in the cavalry was a big deal. Grant's most legendary exploits were with a rough and tumble horse called York.

This was a big animal, and it was said to be difficult to control, save for the best riders. Grant was intrigued, and he made it his mission to tame this beast. And tame it he did. With this belligerent beast of burden, Grant managed to surpass the high-jump record. Grant's feat would not be surpassed for another twenty-five years at the institution.

However, not all of Grant's exploits were as admirable. And as good as he was with horses, it has been said that during his senior year, in March of 1843, there was an instance in which he became so agitated with a horse that he actually gave it a good, solid whack with his saber. Such careless violence from an officer against a horse was considered highly improper. Grant's actions caused him to be punished with what amounted to house arrest—two weeks of seclusion in the barracks.

Nevertheless, he persevered and got through these hard times. Ulysses S. Grant ended up finishing his time at West Point in 1843, and he attended his official graduation ceremony on June 30th of that year. Once he graduated, though, Grant had to figure out what to do next. He went back to Bethel, and shortly after his arrival, he received news from Washington that he had received a commission to be a brevet second lieutenant in the 4th Infantry Regiment. He would soon be posted at the Jefferson Barracks in Missouri.

In the meantime, Grant had some catching up to do back home. He was now a military man, and just the sight of his sharp uniform, with its trim blue, white, and gold fittings, was enough to command attention. But not everyone was so generous—in fact, they maybe were even jealous. At one point during an outing in Cincinnati, a youngster approached Grant. He took one look at his fine uniform and shouted, "Soldier! Will you work? No, sirree—I'll sell my shirt first!"

For a man who would end up leading armies through the most dangerous and rugged of terrains, Grant was notoriously sensitive on a personal level. It is a bit unclear what exactly the gist of the mockery was; perhaps it was a reference to Grant's dress shirt. But whatever the context, the youth's uncouth remarks were enough to ruin this West Point graduate's day. This can be evidenced by the fact that the cruel words can still be quoted. Grant obviously remembered them for the rest of his life.

Grant wanted to be someone, and here this ruffian was trying to burst his bubble. Most would probably just shrug off the abuse for what it was—a jealous young man trying to get under a rival's skin. But Grant tended to take personal attacks very poorly. If openly ridiculed, Grant would be sent spiraling into a moment of introspection in which he would start to question himself.

Making matters worse, when he returned to Bethel, a local troublemaker became even more inventive in his ridicule of Grant by actually putting on a pair of blue pants that he had sewn a white stripe onto. The youth was determined to make a mockery of the recently graduated officer, and he began strutting down the street in what amounted to a mock march, all at the expense of Ulysses S. Grant.

Again, most of us, when provoked by a couple of local troublemakers like this, would probably ask ourselves, "Who are these people? And why would their opinion matter?" They were a couple of nobodies, so their mockery should have meant nothing. However, Grant took their actions hard, almost as if it were someone important declaring that he was no good. And the old taunts of his youth, in which folks said that "Ulysses was Useless," came to the forefront of his mind.

Instead of dismissing the taunts, Ulysses carried them with him. From that moment on, he would claim that such taunts provoked within him "a distaste for military uniform" that he "never recovered from." Interestingly enough, in his later career, Grant would be known to dumb down his uniform, making it as rugged and unpretentious as possible. Rather than strutting in a full officer's uniform, he was likely to wear the most average looking of uniforms, as it was the least likely to get attention.

It seems that it all stemmed from these isolated incidents that made such an impression on him after his graduation. He was mocked for "showing off," so he decided to keep his uniform as low-key as possible in the future. It is amazing how a couple of low-lives like this could influence a great man like Ulysses S. Grant, but this is apparently what happened.

Nevertheless, Grant showed up on time at the Jefferson Barracks in Missouri that fall, just as planned. This military installation was made up of a series of impressive stone structures, which were neatly encircled by a white picket fence. In his role with the 4th Infantry, Grant was part of a unit that consisted of roughly seven thousand troops. Grant would run into many former classmates from West Point here.

He even came across his old roommate from the academy— Frederick T. Dent. Grant would see Dent quite a bit during his stay at Jefferson Barracks. This was a particularly useful friendship since Dent's family was only a few miles away, giving Grant a good home away from home. This second home would also prove to be quite pivotal for his personal future since he ended up marrying one of Frederick Dent's sisters—the striking Julia.

Grant first met Julia in February of 1844 when she was eighteen. He had made it a habit to regularly visit the Dent household, and Julia was a major draw. Although later biographers would claim that Julia was not the most physically attractive woman, Grant seemed to be drawn to her lively personality more than anything else. Julia Dent was outgoing and humorous, and her talkative nature was just the thing that Grant needed to break through his own cold, standoffish exterior.

One other thing about Julia really appealed to the young Ulysses; she happened to know her way around a horse! As it turns out, she was an excellent horse rider. Grant and Julia frequently rode alongside one another, and the couple would quickly bond.

According to Julia, Grant was a daily visitor. The only trouble was his routine visits sometimes made him late for his engagements at the Jefferson Barracks. On one occasion, he was so hesitant to leave his love that he ended up late for dinner in the barrack's mess hall. In the highly regimented barracks, this was a big no-no.

Grant's superior officer—Captain Robert C. Buchanan—had an interesting means of punishing those who dared come down to the mess hall late. He required the tardy individual to purchase a bottle of wine for the entire mess hall to enjoy. As Grant and Julia's relationship advanced, Grant supposedly had to buy more than one bottle of wine before it was all said and done.

Little did Grant know that his whole world would soon abruptly change due to developments on the national stage. The drama centered around Texas. Texas had been part of Mexico, but it boasted a large number of American settlers. These settlers rebelled against Mexican authorities and fought a revolution to become an independent republic. Texas ultimately came out on top, and in the subsequent years, Texas would be a sovereign nation to itself. However, from the very beginning of Texas independence, there were Americans both outside and inside Texas who wanted Texas to join the Union.

There were a couple of reasons why the US was hesitant to accept Texas. For one thing, they did not want to press their luck with Mexico. But even more controversial for the state of the Union was the fact that Texas had slaves. At the time, the United States was made up of "free states," which were primarily in the North, in which slavery was illegal, and "slave states," which were primarily in the South, in which slavery was still allowed.

Everyone knew that Texas would enter the Union as a slave state. The Northern states feared that it would give the Southern states more influence and an advantage over them. As such, many were hesitant to allow Texas to be admitted since doing so would disrupt the delicate balance of power between the free states and the slave states.

Nevertheless, the war drums started to beat, and as tensions between the US and Mexico flared, war was declared. Grant knew that he would be away for a while, so he sought some reassurance for his potential future with Julia. He actually tried to give her his class ring from West Point, informing her that he always wanted to hand the ring off to the woman he intended to marry.

Without directly saying it, Grant was basically proposing that the two start their engagement. But Julia, who was still young and not quite ready for such a big step, found herself taken aback. In a flustered manner, she entirely sidestepped the whole thing by declaring, "Oh no! Mama would never approve of my accepting a gift from a gentleman!"

Julia acted as if it was a simple matter of not wishing to take a gift, but in doing so, she refused to even consider the actual proposal that was being made. Grant, who was already sensitive about his prospects and keen to avoid rejection, was devastated. He was not ready to give up, though. A couple of weeks later, Grant finally came right out and asked the woman he loved if she would marry him. To which she is said to have replied, "It would be charming to be engaged, but married? No! I would rather be engaged."

The answer is a bit puzzling, but it was good enough for Grant. They would be engaged to be married. Julia only had one caveat: she told her newfound fiancé, "Don't tell Papa!" But this time around, Julia did indeed accept Grant's ring.

Chapter 3 – Headed Off to War

"The art of war is simple enough. Find out where your enemy is. Get at him as soon as you can. Strike him as hard as you can, and keep moving on."

-Ulysses S. Grant

After hostilities came to a breaking point with Mexico over America's decision to annex Texas, Ulysses S. Grant found himself headed off to war. In March of 1846, Ulysses S. Grant received his marching orders to head to Fort Texas near the Rio Grande River. The fort had been hastily built in anticipation of an attack by Mexican forces from the other side of the waterway.

The Mexican government, which considered the Nueces River as the rightful border with Texas at the time, considered the mobilization of military force on the Rio Grande as an act of war. Things then came to a head on April 25th, 1846, when the Mexican cavalry arrived on the scene. The men crossed the Rio Grande and launched an assault on some sixty-three dragoons. This attack killed eleven Americans and wounded several others. Those who survived the ordeal were taken as prisoners of war.

Washington had been looking for a reason for war with Mexico, and it had found it. This led to an all-out battle erupting on May 8th between a force of around 2,300 American troops and about 4,000 Mexican soldiers in Palo Alto (near modern-day Brownsville, Texas). The Mexican forces were led by the legendary Santa Anna, a great military strategist who was known as the "Napoleon of the

West."

Santa Anna's larger force was indeed impressive, but their arms were hopelessly outdated compared to the weapons used by the Americans. Grant and his comrades were using powerful artillery, the best rapid-fire rifles, whereas the Mexican troops were stuck with outdated Spanish guns that were slow to load and slow to fire. Unable to withstand the withering gunfire arrayed against them and after losing some three hundred troops in a matter of minutes, the Mexican Army was forced to retreat. The US troops, in the meantime, had only lost five soldiers. Five for three hundred—it was a stunning victory for the Americans and a clear sign of what was to come.

In later years, Grant would come to regret the war, feeling that it was an unjust conflict that bullied the Mexicans out of their land. In the aftermath of the American Civil War in the 1860s, this was a fairly popular view among Republicans like Grant. The war with Mexico had come to be seen as a precursor of the Civil War in the sense that the Southerners' push to annex Texas as a "slave state" put America on a trajectory that would lead to civil strife.

But Grant's views toward the end of his life were likely much different than they were during the war. Although his thoughts at the time were not recorded, this young man must have been fairly enthusiastic since he was caught up in these incredible wars on the ground. At any rate, the Mexican Army regrouped after the Battle of Palo Alto in a place known as the Resaca de la Palma.

Here, the Mexican positions holed up behind a backdrop of thick vegetation and swamps, which denied the pursuing American troops direct access to the Mexicans. There would be no long-range potshots; instead, the terrain ensured that most of the fighting would be up close and personal. The Mexicans hoped that this would neutralize the Americans' technological advantage by forcing them to take part in what amounted to practically hand-to-hand combat with a much larger army.

Grant's unit was one of those that was led through the maze of these swamplands under fire from the Mexicans. At one point, Grant navigated through a couple of ponds and literally led the way, raising his saber and crying out, "Charge!" There would be countless charges into the waiting enemy, but the Americans finally prevailed.

Despite their larger numbers, the Mexican Army fell to pieces when faced with the relentless and tenacious Americans. Soon, the American forces had marched on the Mexican city of Matamoros, and they dug in their heels to occupy the town. By August, Grant had been promoted to the position of quartermaster of his 4th Infantry unit.

Grant was pleased with the pay increase, but he was not happy with the fact that this position took him away from the front lines. Grant wanted to be able to take charge and distinguish himself in battle; being the quartermaster decreased the odds of him being able to do so. Grant was so upset that he actually appealed the decision with a superior officer named Lieutenant Colonel John Garland, demanding that the army reconsider. Grant wrote, "I respectfully protest against being assigned to a duty which removes me from sharing in the dangers and honors of service with my company at the front."

Despite all of his appeals, there was no negotiation. Grant would be quartermaster, and that was that. Grant was picked for the role because of his leadership ability and meticulous attention to detail. The quartermaster was to make sure that the troops were in order and that supplies were at the ready. As part of his role, Grant was sent on scouting missions all over the recently occupied sections of Mexico. He was to be on the lookout for goods and resources that could be requisitioned for the US Army's efforts.

One of the most important goods that Grant requisitioned was a detailed map of Mexico, which he had purchased from a Mexican teamster. It is believed that this teamster had somehow stolen the map from a Mexican general. Due to decades of political instability, Mexico was in a state of constant upheaval, and there was always a black market of illicit goods and underground (possibly stolen) merchandise.

It is not entirely clear how this Mexican teamster got a hold of this map, but it was a top-notch piece of cartography, as it was detailed enough to be used by the Mexican military. It would prove to be a vital tool for the Americans as they pushed deeper into Mexican territory. Grant and company would soon drive some two hundred miles west of Matamoros and began to lay siege to the city of Monterrey.

The Mexican Army was in full force here, and after three days of fighting, there was a tremendous loss of life on both sides. Grant, who was staying true to the role of quartermaster, watched from a distance. That was his role, and those were his orders. But after the third day of seeing his fellow soldiers fight and die in this heated conflict, he could no longer bring himself to follow such a directive.

In one bold moment, he hopped onto his horse and charged right into the heat of the battle. He arrived just in time to find his own unit attempting to mount an attack on the Mexican artillery. Initially, the plan was to launch an assault on this Mexican artillery so that the firepower would be diverted toward the attacking unit, therefore giving cover to the main bulk of the army attempting to enter the city.

Things did not go quite so well, and the unit was repulsed with devastating losses, which included the death of the 4th Infantry's adjutant. Grant was immediately requisitioned to fill in the role of the slain commander. After a couple more days of bloody fighting, the Americans finally breached the city. However, they did not get too far since the Mexican troops, which were holed up in nearby residences, were hitting the Americans with a blistering barrage of fire if they dared to advance.

The Mexican Army appeared to be well stocked in supplies, which stood in stark contrast to the ill-equipped Americans. In fact, many of the troops were becoming dangerously low on ammunition. If the enemy realized how precarious their situation was, it was possible that a sudden massive counter-offensive on their part could have decimated the invading Americans. It was realized that someone needed to get the word out to Major General David Twiggs, who was positioned far from the battlefield, that more supplies were needed.

Grant readily volunteered to ride off to the distant base camp to make this request known. It has been said that Grant rode out of Monterrey while employing one of his favorite tricks in horse riding. With one foot hooked into the side saddle, he stood with his whole body on one side of the horse. He then purposefully rode away from the conflict with only his horse's body exposed to gunfire. This was perhaps smart for a soldier but certainly a bit disconcerting for the horse!

Nevertheless, despite several shots sent his way, both he and the horse were left unscathed. Once Grant was away from the danger of Monterrey, he then rode normally back to the base camp to let them know what was happening. But his trip proved to be futile. While he was gone, a seismic shift had occurred on the battlefield. Both sides were tired and beaten, and after the Americans pulled back, the two sides entered into negotiations with one another.

Although the Mexicans clearly had the upper hand at this stage, as one strong counter-offensive could have possibly defeated the American contingent, the Americans were able to persuade the Mexicans into thinking that their best option would be for both sides to agree to a truce.

As part of the agreement, the Mexican Army was allowed to peacefully depart with all of their weapons and supplies, while the Americans were left to occupy what was left of Monterrey. The American commanders were essentially playing a bluffing game with the Mexican Army. In reality, they knew that if the Mexican military were to unite as one and launch a major unified offensive against them, they would be driven out.

But the Mexican military, like much of Mexican society at the time, was hopelessly fractured. Rather than being able to present one unified force, there were several smaller factions that were either not willing or not able to work together. The forces at Monterrey were just one of these patchwork factions of the Mexican Army.

There were even occasions in which American troops were not exactly sure who they were fighting. Grant himself found this out shortly after the truce when he led a foraging expedition in northern Mexico to requisition some badly needed staple goods for the troops. During this foray, Grant's group was ambushed by a motley crew that seemed to consist of some Mexican troops as well as outright desperadoes and ordinary local townspeople.

Nevertheless, Grant and company fought hard. Although they were outnumbered, they won the day. Grant himself glowingly reported to one of his superior officers, "I lost one man and had a horse wounded. We captured three of the enemy, three horses and a flag, and we had a handsome fight!"

By 1847, however, US President James Polk was looking for a quick end to the conflict. It was then that the military high command determined that the best way to bring a quick and decisive end to the conflict was to take the battle to Mexico's capital—Mexico City. And the best way to march on Mexico City with a limited number of troops and supplies would be to land a force by sea near the shores of Veracruz.

It would be a straight drive to the Mexican capital from there. Grant was part of this invasion force, which landed at Veracruz on March 9th, 1847. Grant, along with his fellow comrades in arms, came to shore aboard so-called "surf boats," which were sent from the main naval craft. It was eerily quiet when they landed. Surprisingly enough, there was no Mexican Army there to greet them.

The main hardship these invaders faced was simply dealing with the elements. Even in March, it was a hot day, and many of the troops had the misery of dealing with sandstorms, with sand relentlessly pelting them in the face and obscuring their vision. Nevertheless, the Americans came ashore and soon wrapped around the port city of Veracruz.

Although they came ashore unopposed, taking the heavily fortified city of Veracruz would not be easy. The Americans made use of their long-range artillery, launching explosive rounds into Mexican positions that were well within the city limits. The Mexicans shot off a blistering array of bullets around the clock. The Americans dug in and did their best to dodge the bombs and bullets being hurled at them.

The siege ultimately lasted for three weeks before the defenders of Veracruz gave up and handed over the keys to their city to the Americans. After solidifying their position at Veracruz, the Americans then marched onward to the inland capital of Mexico—Mexico City. The Mexican Army, which was led by the legendary Santa Anna, rode out to meet the invaders and set up shop some fifty miles from Veracruz.

They dug into their position in the mountainous region, ready to ambush the Americans as soon as they came near. None other than Robert E. Lee would thwart these plans by finding a side route that would allow the Americans to go around the Mexican positions.

It is worth noting that during this conflict, Grant would get to know his later "arch-nemesis" in the American Civil War —Robert E. Lee—quite well. They were acquaintances, and some might even say friends by the time the Mexican-American War ran its course. And as many historians have pointed out, it was this close association from the past that helped smooth over Lee's ultimate surrender to Grant at the end of the American Civil War.

At any rate, this ingenious tactic of Lee's allowed the Americans to launch a surprise attack on the Mexicans who had been sent to surprise attack them! As American troops closed in from behind, the Mexican troops were shocked to suddenly sustain an assault from their back flanks.

In the meantime, Grant was busy making sure the supply lines were in order. Once the fight commenced, he tried to catch up, but he was not able to regroup with the main contingent. Instead, he positioned himself with an artillery battery fielded by Lieutenant George McClellan. From here, all Grant could do was watch the main battle as it unfolded in the distance.

After the Mexican troops began to retreat, Grant and McClellan both decided to charge forward and fight alongside the rest of the Americans. The battle was all but over by the time they arrived on the scene. The army then marched on Mexico City as planned, reaching the gates of this Mexican metropolis that September.

The general in charge of it all, Winfield Scott, was soon making his headquarters inside the famed Hall of Montezuma. This was a feat that helped give rise to the military anthem known as the "Marines' Hymn," which proudly proclaims, "From the Halls of Montezuma/To the shores of Tripoli!"

As for Ulysses S. Grant? For all of his efforts, he was given the rank of first lieutenant. Not bad for a soldier still in his twenties. Mexico ended up suing for peace and signed the Treaty of Guadalupe Hidalgo on February 2nd, 1848. This treaty ceded all land north of the Rio Grande to the United States in exchange for the US paying $15 million in damages and taking on about $3.5 million of Mexico's debts in the region.

Grant was most likely relieved that the war was over. Still, American soldiers were not able to make their way home until that summer. It was already June when Grant made his way to Veracruz, where he and the other soldiers were to disembark for repatriation back to the US.

However, Ulysses S. Grant ran into some mischief along the way when he misplaced a large amount of money. As quartermaster, it was his responsibility to safeguard the quartermaster funds, and he was carrying a sum of about $1,000 in a locked trunk as he journeyed to Veracruz. As Lieutenant DeRussy of the 4th Infantry would later recall about the night of June 16th, 1848, "the trunk containing said funds was stolen from the tent of Capt. Gore, this whilst Capt. Gore and myself were both sleeping in the tent."

No one seemed to know what had happened to the money, but since it was Grant who was in charge of carrying the funds, he was ultimately held responsible. The bill he owed would be a lingering, unpleasant reminder of the war. Nevertheless, Grant made his way to Veracruz and boarded a boat with several other soldiers. They set sail for Pascagoula, Mississippi, arriving on American soil that July.

After acquiring a two-month leave, Grant then made his way back to the arms of his beloved Julia Dent. The two were wed on August 22nd, 1848, in St. Louis, Missouri. Grant knew that wars were lost and wars were won, but as it pertained to him personally, his marriage to his wife was the greatest victory he had ever achieved.

Chapter 4 – Grant's Lonely Outpost

"The friend in my adversity I shall always cherish most. I can better trust those who helped to relieve the gloom of my dark hours than those who are so ready to enjoy with me the sunshine of my prosperity."

-Ulysses S. Grant

Soon after their wedding, Grant received new marching orders. He was to man a post in Detroit. His newly married bride, Julia, was not exactly thrilled with the prospect. She broke down in tears at the thought of leaving the comfortable laidback lifestyle she had with her parents. Her father had a solution: Julia could stay with them, and Grant could simply visit her on leave.

This, of course, would have been a highly abnormal relationship. A military man like Grant should not be forced to go to his post by himself and then travel a great distance while on leave just to see his wife! Grant was frustrated by the suggestion. He asked his wife, "Would you like to remain with your father and let me go alone?" Fortunately for Grant, Julia choked back her tears and agreed to go with him.

The couple left for Grant's new posting as the regimental quartermaster of Fort Detroit in November of 1848. He arrived just in time to receive what appeared to be a puzzling change of plans.

He was told that he had been reassigned to Sackets Harbor, New York. Apparently, the quartermaster who had filled in for Grant refused to leave his post. This quartermaster made it clear that he was not about to uproot himself in the middle of winter.

Due to this, Grant and his wife had to abruptly leave Detroit and head to the post at Sackets Harbor, where they would spend a freezing winter in the full chill that only Lake Ontario can provide. One can only imagine the distress of Julia, who had given up her happy, comfortable life with her parents for this hardship.

In the meantime, Grant lodged a formal complaint with the War Department. By the spring of 1849, it was agreed to send him down to Detroit. Here, the arrangements were a little more conducive for the young couple, and they were able to set up shop in a permanent home of their own. It was a small house in a lower-income section of Detroit, but for the Grants, it was a good enough start. And Grant's job was secure.

It was so secure, in fact, that he found out that there was very little for him to do. He was the quartermaster of a quiet military outpost during peacetime. Most of his job consisted of occasional filling out papers and overseeing the routine drills of soldiers under his charge. But much of his tenure involved a whole lot of nothing, coupled with a constant vigilance just in case something should happen.

There is an old motto in the army: it is a valuable skill to learn how one can "hurry up and wait." Although the expression itself was likely developed after Grant's time (some believe it was coined during World War Two), Grant most certainly learned the gist of it. And he learned it quite well. In many ways, his role at Fort Detroit was a glorified desk job—something which Grant detested. As he would later remark, "I was no clerk, nor had I any capacity to become one."

In the midst of all this boredom, Grant's wife Julia discovered that she was pregnant. This was a joyous occasion, but since Julia decided to finally take her parents up on their offer of room and board—at least for the pregnancy—Grant was left disappointed once again. Julia would later claim that a doctor had specifically told her to go home to St. Louis so that there would not be any complications. But historians have long doubted that she ever received such a recommendation. All the same, Julia no doubt benefited from having her parents and other family members near her to help her through her pregnancy.

At any rate, with the departure of his wife, Ulysses S. Grant was left to fend for himself once again. She would be separated from her husband for about eight months before giving birth to their first child—Frederick Dent Grant—in May of 1850. Grant then obtained a much-needed leave from Detroit and headed off to St. Louis to reunite with his wife and meet his firstborn son.

The young family of three headed back to Detroit that October. It was another cold winter in Detroit, and as it progressed, Grant found himself in an interesting legal spectacle. One day, Grant walked in front of the home of a successful, local businessman by the name of Zachariah Chandler. Chandler had apparently neglected to clear the ice and snow from the sidewalk in front of his home.

Grant stepped on a patch of ice, lost his footing, and fell down. Grant was so incensed by the mishap that he filed a lawsuit against Chandler, suing for injuries sustained from the fall. The official lawsuit described the suit as being due to Chandler failing "to keep his sidewalk free and clear from snow and ice." This case went to trial, and Grant actually won.

But it seems the jury was upset over the pettiness of the lawsuit, so they made sure that the damages awarded to Grant were equally petty. In the end, Chandler was ordered to pay six cents to Grant—which was a minuscule amount of money even back in the 1800s! Grant was also forced to be subjected to public ridicule during the course of the proceedings, with Chandler basically accusing him of being a drunk. At one point, Chandler railed, "If you soldiers would keep sober—perhaps you would not fall on people's pavements and hurt your legs!"

It is unclear if Grant was drunk at the time, but in truth, he had picked up a regular drinking habit that would follow him for the rest of his life. It is believed that he had developed a soft spot for liquor during his days in the Mexican-American War, and he was frequently seen with booze thereafter.

Interestingly enough, Chandler would later become a senator, and he actually managed to become a part of the future President

Grant's cabinet as the secretary of the interior. Both men showed that they could let bygones be bygones. Apparently, they both laughed about the incident later in life and viewed each other good-naturedly from there on out.

As it pertains to the winter of 1850, however, Grant was not too pleased with either the verdict of the Detroit jury or his superior officers. Soon after this, he learned that he would have to pack once again, as he would be headed back to Sackets Harbor, New York. Julia, for one, made it clear that if Grant went, she was not going to join him. She cited the unbearable cold as her reason to stay behind. She and her young son left Grant to stay with her parents, forcing the disillusioned husband and father to head off to his lonely outpost in Sackets Harbor by himself.

Grant would write to his wife frequently to see how things were going, mainly to check on his son, who he often referred to offhandedly as "the little dog." But as much as Grant wanted to keep in touch with what was happening with his wife and child, her perceived lack of interest in readily replying left him depressed and frustrated.

At one point, she went several weeks without saying a word, prompting Grant to snap. "After a lapse of more than one month—I at length received a letter from you yesterday. I do not see that you had any excuse whatever for not writing before." He then sternly warned her, "Do not neglect to write for so long a time again." But no matter how much Grant voiced his frustrations with his wife, she not only tended to take them in stride but also ignored them. Her correspondence to him would remain infrequent.

Grant, in the meantime, passed the summer months of 1851 by making trips to outlying regions when he could. At one point, he even took an excursion to Montreal.

By the following fall, he finally managed to get his wife and child to join him in Sackets Harbor. The reunion was pleasant enough, but it was brief. By the time winter had arrived, Julia had discovered that she was pregnant once again. This gave her all the excuse she needed, and she was soon off to St. Louis once again. It was in the cold and lonely isolation of Sackets Harbor that Grant's drinking took a turn for the worse.

In fact, his drinking habit had become bad enough that he sought an intervention. Fortunately for him, there was help to be found. He joined a local lodge called the Sons of Temperance. He showed up at weekly meetings held in the local Presbyterian church. The group not only helped him to control his drinking habit but also provided a much-needed social outlet for Grant. Grant was soon a full-fledged member of the lodge, and he participated in all of the lodge's events.

Although Grant's penchant for alcohol would come back to haunt him later, at this point in his life, he was happy to put it to the side. At any rate, Grant managed to get through that dark winter.

In the spring of 1852, Grant was given new marching orders. He was told that he would be headed for a military outpost in California. Upon hearing this news, Julia actually offered to head off with her husband for a change. But Grant thought that the trip would be too bothersome for a woman who was about to give birth, so he actually told her to stay behind.

It was indeed a long, complicated trip. It was not just an excursion overland. It involved Grant getting on a boat in New York Harbor and then sailing all the way to the thin strip of land between South America and North America known as the Panama isthmus. This isthmus was then crossed on land to the Pacific. There, Grant got on another ship and sailed right up to the California coast. Making use of the isthmus as a shortcut to the Pacific Ocean was perhaps quicker than a straight shot overland, but it certainly did not make the trip any less arduous or dangerous since both accidents and sickness at sea were quite common.

It seems that soon after setting sail, Grant put aside his previous decision to abstain from alcohol, as he was quite frequently seen with a bottle in his hand. The booze no doubt helped him ease both the boredom and rigors of the trip. Grant also drank alcohol simply to avoid drinking cholera-infected water. There had been several outbreaks among passengers at the time. It is possible that Grant sought to avoid sickness by simply partaking of wine rather than water.

Upon reaching Panama, Grant and company trekked overland the remaining thirty-five miles to the other side of the isthmus so that they could hop on a ship to take them to the Pacific coast of

California. This was before the creation of the Panama Canal, of course, so this overland excursion was the only way Panama could be crossed. The overland trek, though short, was a hard one due to the rugged terrain, tropical heat, and the frequent outbreak of disease.

Considering all of this, Grant was most likely correct in his assumption that his wife would be best left at home. The journey was dangerous enough for a man in full, perfect health, so it certainly would not have been easy for someone like Julia, who was heavily pregnant at the time. Nevertheless, Grant and his fellow soldiers made their way to the other side of the Panama isthmus on July 26th, 1852.

By then, several of the men who had accompanied him had perished along the way. Most of them had succumbed to the aforementioned cholera outbreak. It is indeed amazing what Grant and his peers had to go through simply to cross one side of America to the other. The incident would stick with Grant. Upon becoming president, he urged Congress of the need to create "a path between the seas." It was musings like this that would eventually lead to the construction of the Panama Canal, which would allow ships to pass from one side of the continent to the other without their passengers having to disembark on a dangerous overland route.

Nevertheless, Grant was able to board the ship waiting to take him to California—the Golden Gate. This freighter took him and his fellow survivors from the west coast of Panama to the west coast of California, arriving in August of 1852.

Grant landed in San Francisco, which at that time was comprised of around fifty thousand people. The city was small by today's standards, but it was still a wild metropolis in its own right back then—and that fifty thousand had arrived at a rapid rate. Many souls came during the 1848 Gold Rush, which created a hectic mix of hopeful newcomers ready to strike it rich.

Ulysses S. Grant ended up settling in at a town called Benicia, which was some fifteen miles north of San Francisco. There, he took some time to recover from the rigors of his previous journey. Grant's wife Julia had given birth to their second son in the meantime and named him after their father, christening the child Ulysses Jr.

Grant desperately yearned for his family to join him, but a reunion was not yet in the cards. Instead, once he felt better, he hopped on a steamboat and sailed up to Fort Vancouver, which was located some eight miles north of Portland, Oregon. Grant had a lot of downtime there, and he proceeded to use it to pursue various schemes to make money. His first enterprise was to partner with a merchant by the name of Elijah Camp to set up a general store in the vicinity of Fort Vancouver. The store was a success, but Elijah Camp managed to convince Grant into selling his share of the business. Grant was able to make $1,500 by doing so.

However, Grant would soon regret his decision, as he later realized that if he had kept his co-ownership of the store, he could have made as much as $3,000 every year. Nevertheless, Grant moved on to his next money-making scheme. He wanted to get into the potato market since he realized that one could make $8 a bushel for this in-demand bit of produce.

In order to make this enterprise happen, he hooked up with a local farmer by the name of Ogden. He let Grant use his land for farming if Grant worked on the fencing on the property. It was certainly enough to keep him busy. Ogden's property was sprawling, and on top of that, Grant had to tend to his budding potatoes on the farm. He was successful in growing a massive crop of potatoes, but unfortunately for him, the demand for them dropped just as soon as he was ready to sell them.

By the time harvest time came around, it seemed as if just about everyone in the San Francisco Bay area had the same idea as him. The market was absolutely flooded with potatoes. This massive supply brought down demand, and it, in turn, sunk the price from eight dollars a bushel to approximately twenty-five cents. In the end, Grant did not even make enough money to cover the expenses racked up from tending the farm.

This business failure was followed by another when he attempted to start selling logs, which was then followed by a failed pig farm. Soon after that, Grant went into the hotel business, leasing space with some fellow officers in the San Francisco area. This was the one enterprise that seemed to be successful—that is, until the manager put on Grant's payroll suddenly decided to skip town with all of the money that had been made.

It seemed that whatever Grant tried to invest his time, money, and effort into was an abject failure. In the midst of this misery, Grant was again transferred, this time to Fort Humboldt in the northern reaches of California. That fall, he was promoted to captain. It should have been a happy moment, but all Grant felt was despair.

He was over a thousand miles from his wife, who was raising children who he barely knew. All he wanted to do was get back to them. Grant just could not take the separation any longer, and so, at thirty-two years of age when most had firmly settled into their military careers, Grant made the fateful decision to give it all up and resign.

Chapter 5 – Living a Hardscrabble Life

"My failures have been errors in judgment, not of intent."

-Ulysses S. Grant

After submitting his resignation, Grant borrowed some money from his friend and fellow West Point alum Simon Bolivar Buckner (who would fight in the Civil War on the Confederate side) and headed off to reunite with his family in St. Louis. Grant went back the same way he had; it was not an easy journey. He sailed to Panama and once again crossed the Panama isthmus before sailing to New York. After an exhausted and nearly broke Ulysses S. Grant reached a hotel in New York, he contacted both his wife and his parents to let them know of his whereabouts.

Jesse's father back in Ohio was absolutely appalled when he heard of what his son had done. Upon learning of his son's resignation, he immediately sent out a letter to the secretary of war—Jefferson Davis—to ask for his son's reinstatement. Yes, the future president of the Confederacy, Jefferson Davis, was the same man who was the secretary of war when Grant tendered his resignation.

Jesse pleaded with Davis, explaining that his son had made a rash decision under the duress of being separated from his family. He asked Davis to give him a six-month furlough instead so that he could go back to his post afterward. Davis was no help, stating that it was too late, and refused to intercede on Ulysses's behalf.

Grant made his way from New York to his parents' homestead in Covington. After a distressing reunion with his worried parents, he then made his way to St. Louis, Missouri, to see his wife and kids. It has been said that when Ulysses pulled up at the Dent family homestead, his two sons were playing out front and ran away when their father approached. To them, he was just a stranger.

After this strange reunion with his wife and children, Grant and his family were allowed to stay at a house that Julia's brother Louis had constructed on the family property. However, Grant did not like living under someone else's roof, so he decided to literally build his own roof.

In the spring of 1855, he built a simple, modest house that he and his family would call home, at least for a time. He cut down trees, fashioned the wood, built doors and the chimney, and installed the windows. It was not easy, and he named the place appropriately, calling it his "hardscrabble" estate.

Grant, who had financial help from his father Jesse, then began to start his own farm on the homestead. Along with raising crops, he also sold firewood to make extra money. Another source of revenue was through renting out his horse. It was indeed a hardscrabble existence, but two things made Grant happy, even in the midst of his hardship—being near his family and being able to keep busy.

Previously, Grant had been drowning in despair, sitting at a military barracks, lonely and with nothing to do. Now, he had enough on his plate to keep him occupied all day long, and at the end of the day, he had a wife and kids to come home to. And his family was growing. His wife Julia gave birth to his third child, a daughter named Ellen, on July 4th, 1855. Grant was overjoyed to be a father again.

Even so, life on the farm would soon prove to be too much for Grant. He worked his fingers to the bone, and he developed bad arthritis as a result. Making matters worse, he had recurring bouts of malaria symptoms, an illness he first came down with on his way back from California. Julia was not liking life at "Hardscrabble" either. And just a few months into this experiment, she found an excuse to extricate the family from the homestead.

Her mother passed away, and she was able to make the case that she and Grant should move the family back into her dad's house under the guise of looking after him. So, that was what they did. Grant managed to rent out the Hardscrabble house to someone, and they headed off to Mr. Dent's estate. The experience would prove to be quite miserable for Grant.

His father-in-law, the "southern gentleman," had always viewed his "Yankee" son-in-law with a certain degree of contempt even before he quit the army. And now that he was perceived as a drop-out with dismal financial prospects, Dent looked down on Grant all the more. His previous disdain, which had been carefully masked, was now out in the open.

In the fall of 1857, the US entered a bad economic recession. Life for almost everyone became just a little more difficult and frustrating. By the time the holiday season arrived, Grant found himself unable to buy even the cheapest of Christmas gifts. In order to raise some cash, he was forced to sell his gold watch. Complicating matters even further, by the following spring, Grant had another mouth to feed. His youngest child, Jesse, was born on February 6th, 1858. The baby was named in honor of Grant's father.

The family would struggle on. The situation would not improve much in the next couple of years, and by the spring of 1860, Grant finally accepted his own father's offers of help. Jesse had been trying to get Grant to move up to Galena, Illinois, to work in his prospering leather business. With no other prospects in life, Grant finally answered the call. He rented out a modest, seven-room home for his family and set to work to become his father's apprentice.

It was quite a turnaround for Grant. As a young man, he had sworn to his father that he would not go into business with him. But now, as he approached middle age, he was attempting to do just that. He was essentially a low-level clerk. Even more humiliating, he was under the supervision of his younger brothers—Simpson and Orvil. The scrutiny was high, the pay was mediocre, and the work was boring. Everyone knew that Grant's heart was not in it. But he had no choice.

In the meantime, the nation as a whole was becoming increasingly tense over the issue of slavery. The Southern states supported the Democratic Party, which in those days was supportive of slavery, whereas the North was becoming increasingly supportive of the Republican Party, which advocated for ending the practice or at least placing more limitations on it. By the time of the election of 1860, the Republicans had nominated Abraham Lincoln, a critic of slavery, while the Democrats ended up with two candidates—Stephen A. Douglas and John C. Breckinridge. Democrat candidate Breckinridge was an outright supporter of slavery, while Stephen A. Douglas was viewed as a more moderate Democrat.

The political situation was a primary topic of conversation in Jesse's leather shop. As Grant packaged leather goods for customers, he was more often than not likely to hear some of the latest talk on the upcoming election. Grant himself was unable to vote since he had not been in the state of Illinois long enough to meet the residency requirement.

Nevertheless, even if he did not actually cast a ballot, he supported the moderate Democrat Stephen Douglas, although he admired Lincoln. Part of his reasoning for sticking with the Democratic Party was due to the fact that his wife's family was staunchly Democrat. Grant also knew that if Lincoln, an anti-slavery Republican, was elected, the slave-holding Democrats of the South would be so infuriated that they just might rebel.

Grant knew that this threat was real, as the tensions had been simmering for some time. From his experience back in St. Louis, he had heard open talk of such things firsthand. As Grant would reflect many years later, "It made my blood run cold to hear friends of mine, southern men, discuss dissolution of the Union as though it were a tariff bill."

It was indeed terrible to contemplate how easily chaos might erupt, but Grant was right. And before Abraham Lincoln was even sworn in, Grant's fear became a reality. The states of the South—starting with South Carolina—began to secede from the Union one by one. These states would join forces and become the Confederate States of America (CSA). They appointed former Secretary of War Jefferson Davis as their president.

The rightful president of the United States, Abraham Lincoln, was sworn in that March. He had quite a bit on his plate, to say the least. Lincoln wished to avoid war if it were possible, so he avoided direct military action in the first month of his administration. It was only when Confederate troops attacked a federally run fort in South Carolina—Fort Sumter—on April 12th, 1861, that President Lincoln knew that bloodshed was unavoidable. The Civil War had begun.

Chapter 6 – The Civil War Begins

"Everyone has his superstitions. One of mine has always been when I started to go anywhere, or to do anything, never to turn back or to stop until the thing intended was accomplished."

-Ulysses S. Grant

On April 16th, 1861, Ulysses S. Grant was seated at a town meeting at the local courthouse in Galena. The townspeople, just like practically everyone else in the nation, were on edge. They were frantic for news of what was happening and struggling to figure out what action they—if any—should take in the face of this oncoming storm.

The mayor of Galena was actually a Democrat, and although he was shocked at what was happening, he at first attempted to sympathize with his fellow Democrat Southern secessionists. He agreed that leaving the Union was wrong under any circumstances, but he pleaded that brother shouldn't fight brother. He openly pleaded for a way to push back the tides of war.

The Republican congressman of the district was there as well, and predictably enough, he called everyone to arms to protect the Union and stop the secessionists. It was a twenty-nine-year-old local attorney named John A. Rawlins, however, who really stole the show. Grant knew Rawlings because he had worked for his father in the past.

Rawlings was a life-long Democrat, but the idea that states would actually leave the Union infuriated him. He spoke about his opinions to the crowd that gathered in that courthouse that day. He proclaimed, "I have been a Democrat all my life. But this is no longer a question of politics. It is simply union or disunion, country or no country. I have favored every honorable compromise, but the day for compromise is past. Only one course is left for us. We will stand by the flag of our country and appeal to the god of battles to vindicate our flag!"

It remains unclear exactly what "god of battles" the man might have been referring to, but the folks at the courthouse got the point. Soon, they were shouting and providing a lively chorus to his call for war. And although Grant may not have been quite as vociferous in his expression of it, he was among them. At that moment, Grant came to accept that a war to save the Union must be fought.

President Lincoln issued an order for seventy-five thousand able-bodied men to sign up for service in their local militias for a term that would supposedly last just a few months. This surge of volunteers was needed to compensate the official US Army, which at that time consisted of only around seventeen thousand troops. The troops of the Union were finite, and even the seventeen thousand who made up the official army were scattered across the nation.

For example, many had been sent west to man lonely outposts in the newly gained lands on the Pacific coast. It would take some time before they could regroup to face the threat of the Confederate Army, which was primarily centered in the southeast of the country. It was for this reason that volunteers from state-run militias were so crucial in defending the Union.

Although Grant had resigned from the military, he now had the perfect opportunity to put on a fighting uniform once again. Ulysses S. Grant's newly adopted state of Illinois was asking for a total of six volunteer regiments. This led to the town of Galena rushing to hold a session in which to recruit men. Local Congressman Elihu B. Washburne, who knew of Grant's prior experience, saw to it that Grant presided over the discussion.

It was made known among the group that they wished for Grant to become the captain of the local militia, but he declined the responsibility. He still held out hope that he might somehow be able to return to the regular army. Nevertheless, he agreed to train and serve as a recruiter for the local militia.

On April 25th, Galena saw its very first unit of militia members assemble together in their dark blue and grey uniforms. These men were sent to the train depot, where they disembarked for Springfield. This was where the other local militias had gathered. One Ulysses S. Grant was among them. Grant had attempted to lobby the military to be reenlisted in the regular army, but his reinstatement was rejected.

However, with the support of Congressman Elihu B. Washburne, on April 29th, he was given the role of military aide to Illinois Governor Richard Yates. This meant a return to the boring deskwork that Grant loathed, as he had to fill out forms and keep track of inventory. But at $2 a day, he was simply glad it paid him well enough to get by.

Still, Grant held out hope that he could somehow be reinstated back into the regular army as an officer. Little did Grant know that Governor Yates was already hearing plenty of negative remarks about Grant from others. He was mercilessly referred to as a quitter and a deadbeat. The instance during the Mexican-American War in which he somehow let $1,500 get away from him as quartermaster was frequently mentioned as a reason to avoid Grant's reinstatement.

However, Grant would not give up. On May 24th, he went right over the governor of Illinois's head by writing a letter directly to the adjutant general in DC. He wrote the man, pleading to be given charge of one of the recently cobbled together infantry units on account of his previous experience.

In the letter, he wrote, "I would say that in view of my present age, and length of service, I feel myself competent to command a regiment." He was direct and to the point. It was indeed a simple enough request, but it would be left unanswered. Disillusioned, Grant drifted aimlessly for the next couple of months, seeking purpose. His luck was about to change when one of Illinois's regiments proved to be so disorderly and unruly that it needed a truly gifted hand at the helm.

It was then that Governor Yates began to reconsider Grant. And to Grant's great joy, on June 15th, he was informed that he had been selected to head the disorderly 21st Illinois Regiment, not as a volunteer captain but as an official colonel of the US Army. Grant would get his reinstatement after all.

Grant jumped at the chance. And although others would have been hesitant to command such a drunken, loudmouth bunch as the 21st Regiment was at the time, Grant had no fear. Just like the crazed and wild horses he had tamed in his youth, he was confident that he would eventually gain mastery over this unruly bunch as well. He believed they would soon fall in line under his calm, steady gaze. It would not be easy, but he would figure it out as he went along.

His crew was indeed a motley one. They did not even have uniforms. Most were in their work clothes, as they had come straight from the farm or the factory. Grant himself had no uniform save the beaten and battered rags he had saved from before his resignation from the military several years prior.

Nevertheless, Grant was ready to whip these men into shape. His quiet demeanor belied a real ruthlessness when he was in charge. Grant immediately made it clear that he would not tolerate any insubordination. Anyone who disagreed would be tied to a post until they decided to behave. He even had some of these men gagged in order to teach them from using profanity in his presence.

Grant was a real taskmaster, and it was amazing how he worked these men. And he soon had them falling in line. The regiment was officially sworn in on June 28th and then sent marching off to Quincy, Illinois. And when we say marching, we literally mean *marching*. Grant led the men directly on the ground as they made their way across the expanse of Illinois, traveling at a pace of about one hundred miles a week.

Grant knew from experience that such a task was good for the morale of the troops because it forced them to work together under hardship. The men learned how to walk with their heavy equipment and guns without missing a beat. Short of actually fighting in a battle, going on a long march overland was great for building up much-needed solidarity and discipline.

Grant was beaming with pride over his troops once they made it to Quincy. After looking his men over, he even went as far as to proclaim that they behaved as if they were "veteran troops in point of soldierly bearing, general good order, and cheerful execution of commands." Although these new recruits did well enough, equating them to "veteran troops" was perhaps laying it on a little thick.

Nevertheless, Grant wanted his men to know that he approved of their efforts. After their short stay in Quincy, Grant had his men march across the Illinois border with Missouri. In the northeast corner of Missouri, his regiment had its first assignment. They were to sniff out any potential Confederate guerrillas who might be lurking about and sabotaging bridges and rail lines.

Such things were indeed common enough during the war, so the idea of finding Confederates or Confederate sympathizers damaging federal property was not a far-fetched prospect. Things became serious when the group reached Palmyra, Missouri. Grant received orders to send them in pursuit of a large group of Rebels (another name for the Confederates) that were being commanded by Confederate General Thomas A. Harris.

Just before the first great challenge of the regiment, Grant began to have serious doubts. He was not fearful of his own life but rather the lives of those under his charge. He was now the leader of men, and he most certainly did not want to lead them all to early graves. The responsibility he had was beginning to weigh quite heavily on him. Nevertheless, he took a breath and prepared himself to lead his troops into battle.

But in this instance, the battle never arrived. They ended up finding General Harris's camp, but it was already deserted. Harris and company had apparently been tipped off that Grant and his men were coming, and they had decided to take off. Grant concluded that despite his misgivings, the Confederate troublemakers were apparently much more afraid of his advance than he was of confronting them. As Grant would later put it, "It occurred to me at once that Harris was much more afraid of me as I had been of him. This was a view of the question that I had never taken before; but it was one I never forgot afterwards."

The larger war was heating up, though. On July 21st, 1861, the Union Army suffered a terrible defeat at the Battle of Bull Run.

The battle was just a short distance from the capital, and if the Confederates had pressed on, they might have threatened the White House. However, the Union Army ended up holding its ground, and the crisis was temporarily averted.

In the meantime, Grant received a promotion, reaching the rank of brigadier general on August 5th. In stark contrast to his days wasting away at lonely, remote military outposts, Grant was now right in the thick of things. Finally, his hard work was being recognized.

Grant and company were given new marching orders on August 7th. Grant was informed that his men were to head to his old stomping grounds of Jefferson Barracks. Plans abruptly changed, as they tend to do during wars, and Grant and his unit were sent off to Ironton, Missouri, instead.

This area was important for its industrial capacity, and it had reportedly been in danger of an attack by a group of Confederates. Grant immediately rushed his men over there, managing to cover some 110 miles in less than 24 hours' time. Upon his arrival, Grant was handed over a bit of intelligence, which stated that a large contingent of Rebel forces was getting ready to congregate in the low hills in the vicinity of Ironton.

Knowledge of being potentially outnumbered by a larger group of fighters could be a source of intimidation for anyone, but Grant kept his head. He plumbed the depths of his brain for a solid strategy, and he realized that success would require a good cavalry. This way, he could have men ready to mount their horses and scour the area for any interlopers headed their way.

He also knew that he needed to have some heavy artillery in place just in case a major standoff took place. Although the potential for trepidation was there, Grant told himself that the Confederate forces were no better trained or equipped than his and that they were likely just as fearful. If push did come to shove, Grant was confident that his unit could stand its ground.

Chapter 7 – Ready for Anything

"I appreciate the fact, and am proud of it, that the attentions I am receiving are intended more for our country than for me personally."

-*Ulysses S. Grant*

Grant and his men were ready for war in Ironton, but that is not what they got. After getting in place and preparing to be attacked, they learned that the Confederate forces had decided to take off. It was still early in the war for sure, but at this point, Grant must have lost any respect he might have had for the courage of the Confederates. To him, they seemed like a bunch of thugs launching hit-and-run attacks.

As soon as Grant heard that the Confederates were on the run, he made a conscious decision not to let them go. He wanted to send his troops in pursuit of them. It was not meant to be since the high command had other plans.

Grant's plans of pursuit were halted by none other than Brigadier General Benjamin M. Prentiss, a major player in the Battle of Shiloh. The brigadier general suddenly appeared at Grant's base camp and informed him that he had been reassigned by Major General John C. Fremont to southeastern Missouri.

Grant obviously did not like this decision, and he also felt he had a valid point of protest against it. Ulysses S. Grant knew that he outranked Prentiss because, although they were both brigadier generals for the militia, he was a captain in the regular army. This meant that he had seniority and that he trumped Prentiss. This, therefore, gave him a valid legal argument as it pertains to military protocol to argue against this decision. He sent his appeal to the War Department before heading off to Major General John Fremont's headquarters to report to him in person.

Grant presented his argument to Fremont in person, but Fremont did not agree. Fremont ended up ordering Grant to head over to a post in Jefferson City. Grant did not like this and asked to head back to Galena instead. This request was refused, so Grant was sent off to Jefferson City just as Fremont had intended.

But it would be a short stay. Just one week after his arrival, the War Department heard Grant's case and agreed with his argument that he had seniority over Prentiss. This indicated that there was a violation of military protocol, just as Grant had claimed. Fremont tried to make up for this slight by sending Grant to Cairo, Illinois. This city, which is located in southern Illinois, was a strategic stronghold. It put Grant in control of southern Illinois, as well as southeastern Missouri. Upon his arrival, Grant set up shop in an old bank building near the intersection of the Ohio and Mississippi Rivers.

At his new command post, Grant received some intelligence that the Confederates were going to march on Paducah, Kentucky. At that time, Kentucky was neutral, and the Union wanted to keep it that way. In order to prevent a Confederate takeover, something had to be done. Grant immediately rallied his troops and prepared to converge on Paducah, sending Fremont a telegram, stating simply, "I am getting ready to go to Paducah. Will start at 6 ½ o'clock."

As the evening wore on, Grant was still waiting for a response from Fremont. Grant eventually lost his patience waiting for Fremont's approval. He proclaimed to a military aide of his, "Come on. I can wait no longer. I will go if it costs me my commission." And Grant meant what he said; he had four artillery pieces put on three separate steamboats, along with a group of some 1,500 men under his command.

Grant's steamboats reached Paducah around eight in the morning, and he was able to take the town with ease. Although the

Union was essentially an occupying force in a neutral Kentucky town, Grant presented himself and his comrades as liberators. He stood before all who would hear and proclaimed, "I have come among you, not as an enemy but as your friend and fellow citizen, not to injure or annoy you, but to defend and enforce the rights of all loyal citizens. I am here to defend you. I have nothing to do with opinions. I shall deal only with armed rebellion. The strong arm of the government is here to protect its friends, and to punish only its enemies."

Grant then left Brigadier General C. F. Smith in charge of the town and headed back up to Cairo, Illinois. Ironically enough, Grant finally received Fremont's response upon his return. Fremont instructed him to go ahead and proceed to Paducah "if you feel strong enough." Grant was glad that he had seized the moment when he could rather than waiting around for Fremont's weak-willed and delayed response.

Grant would become a much more decisive commander on the field after this venture. He relied more on his own instincts to make last-minute decisions, whether his superior officers agreed to it or not.

Fremont, in the meantime, managed to upset his own superior officer—President Abraham Lincoln. He did so by taking a heavy hand against the citizens of Paducah. Even though Grant had just proclaimed that the Union was their liberator and protector, Fremont took a draconian stance and sought to seize the lands of perceived Confederate sympathizers.

President Lincoln did not wish to alienate the populations of neutral states like Kentucky, so he told Fremont to take back his stringent measures. Fremont refused, and as a result, he was stripped of his authority. Grant was now under the direct oversight of Major General Henry W. Halleck instead. Halleck wanted to take a cautious but proactive approach. That November, he had Grant take his men and march them up and down the Mississippi River in an obvious show of force to deter the Confederates.

Grant did not want to simply deter the enemy; he was ready to take the fight to them. And so when he saw his opportunity, he struck. He led about three thousand troops to the town of Belmont, where a Confederate force had set up an encampment. Grant and his men were able to drive the Confederates out, but as soon as the surprise of the attack wore off, the Confederates were able to regroup.

They struck back at Grant and company. They had a larger force, and it became clear that Grant would have to lead his troops in a tactical retreat. He and his men were able to quickly board the steamboats and race back up the river with minimal losses.

Halleck was not exactly pleased with Grant's modification of his orders, but Grant described the operation as a successful raid and minimized the risk enough that Halleck ultimately decided to let it go. And after giving it some thought, Halleck decided to unleash Grant on a new target—Fort Henry in Tennessee.

This Confederate fort situated on the Cumberland River had been ripe for the picking for some time, and Halleck allowed Grant to be the commander to direct a siege against it. Time was of the essence since the Union had just found out that the Confederate commander, P. G. T. Beauregard, was marching straight toward the fort with fifteen regiments. Grant needed to take the fort before these Confederate reinforcements arrived.

In February of 1862, Grant took his men to Paducah, Kentucky, which they would use as a forward outpost to launch the strike against Fort Henry. Here, he amassed twenty-three regiments, which were comprised of some seventeen thousand troops. All of these men and their equipment would be placed on riverboats to sweep down upon the fort.

One thing that gave the Union troops a serious advantage was the fact that Fort Henry was constructed on low ground. This meant that as the riverboats came downriver, the fortress could be easily bombarded. Confederate forces tried to compensate for this by establishing another fortress on the other side of the river, an outpost they dubbed Fort Heiman.

This fortress was situated a little higher up on the riverbank, but it was so poorly defended that it would prove to make very little difference. In the end, the Confederates knew they did not stand a chance and promptly surrendered on February 6th, 1862, after being waylaid by a squadron led by naval commander Andrew H. Foote.

With Fort Henry under his control, Grant then sent his troops to pacify the nearby Confederate outpost of Fort Donelson, which was farther down the Cumberland River. The fort was shelled by riverboats on February 14th. Shortly after this, on February 16th, the besieged fortress surrendered to the Union troops. This surrender helped to pave a path toward Confederate-controlled Tennessee, and it is considered one of the Union's first major breakthroughs of the war.

In the following month of March, the victorious General Grant found himself leading a robust and strong group of forty thousand troops even deeper into the Confederate strongholds of the South. Immediately under his leadership were a couple of rather colorful officers—Lew Wallace and William Tecumseh Sherman.

Sherman was a brigadier general, but he was sometimes viewed as a loose cannon by the top brass. Nevertheless, he, like Grant, would rise to the top with his daring exploits during the Civil War. Lew Wallace, on the other hand, would become famous for his later role as the governor of New Mexico and his run-ins with Billy the Kid. As these brave and unique men marched south, they became the centerpieces of the incredible drama that was about to unfold.

Chapter 8 – The Battle of Shiloh and Its Aftermath

"I have nothing to do with opinions. I deal only with armed rebellion and its aiders and abettors."

-Ulysses S. Grant

Grant and his men had led several successful expeditions against the Confederates by the spring of 1862, but their first real battle was just before them. This first real test presented itself on April 6th, 1862. The previous day, over forty thousand Confederate troops had made their way within Union lines. Both sides began to take potshots at each other. It was as if both sides were actively testing the mettle of the other right before the main event was about to commence.

Early the next morning, Confederate General Albert Sidney Johnston sent his troops storming into the Union line, kicking off what would be known as the Battle of Shiloh. It was named as such because it was within sight of Shiloh Church. The Confederates took the Union soldiers by surprise and are said to have come down on the Union troops like an "avalanche."

In fact, Grant was taking his first cup of coffee and enjoying some breakfast when he and his chief of staff, Colonel Joseph Webster, heard the unmistakable sound of cannon fire from farther down the river. After briefly discussing the matter, Grant put aside his breakfast and proclaimed to all within earshot, "Gentlemen, the ball is in motion. Let's be off."

By the time Grant's steamboat reached Pittsburg Landing on the Tennessee River's western bank, it was a little after nine o'clock in the morning. The battle was already well underway. Grant could hear the sounds of the battle, a steady stream of gunshots and agonized cries of grown men filling the air. The 53rd Ohio Infantry Regiment was out front, taking the brunt of the assault.

Grant managed to reach General Sherman's position at 10 a.m., but by then, the 53rd had been all but decimated. This loss forced Sherman to command the rest of the troops to take evasive action and withdraw toward the banks of the Tennessee River. Confederate General Johnston was attempting to throw everything he had at the Union troops so that they could break through the Union ranks. Grant, in the meantime, reminded his own troops that they had to hold the line at all cost. And they did.

Ulysses S. Grant was a tireless taskmaster in these efforts. He rode from one part of the defensive line to the other, encouraging soldiers to go on. At times, he more directly coerced those who proved hesitant to fight, telling them to get back to the front. Grant's superb horsemanship was no doubt on display as he daringly rode up and down the line of Union troops, dodging bullets as he went.

It is said that at one point, a staff officer, who was obviously worried about Grant's safety, tried to warn him to flee. Fearing the certain collapse of the Union line, the officer told Grant, "General, we must leave this place. It isn't necessary to stay here. If we do, we shall all be dead in five minutes." These are some pretty sobering words, to be sure, but Grant, after a pause, merely acknowledged the possibility by replying, "I guess that's so."

The Union troops were not the only ones facing the threat of sudden death. A large number of Confederate fighters were cut down as well. During the terrible melee that ensued, even Confederate General Johnston ended up getting killed. Johnston was shot in the leg, and he initially believed it just to be a trivial flesh wound. He was in discomfort but would survive—or at least so he thought.

The bullet was more than a flesh wound. It had torn through his femoral artery, and it would cause him to literally bleed to death on the spot. With his abrupt passing, the direction of the Confederate forces fell on one General Pierre Gustave Toutant-Beauregard (P. G. T. for short). Interestingly enough, Johnston and Beauregard had disagreed on the strategy prior to the attack. Beauregard had not favored waging such a risky assault.

So, after Beauregard took over, his own doubts seemed to pass to all the other troops around him, and the advance soon began to slow. The Union troops, which were initially on the run, were able to rally. In a spot dubbed the "Hornet's Nest," they fought to hold their ground.

The group of Union troops struggling to fend off the Confederates at the Hornet's Nest was being led by Benjamin Prentiss. These defenders were hit by heavy artillery, and they were practically blasted into smithereens by the Confederates. After several hours of this terrific onslaught, Prentiss was forced to acknowledge defeat. What remained of his unit were then captured and made prisoners of war.

Nevertheless, even with the capture of this division, the Confederates proved unable to further penetrate what has since been called "Grant's Last Line" of defense. Grant was questioned at the time about whether or not the Union defense would hold up, and his words would prove fairly prophetic. With the sun setting across the horizon, Grant confidently stated, "They can't break our lines tonight. It's too late. Tomorrow we shall attack them with fresh troops and drive them, of course."

The Confederates were indeed forced to call off their assault. And after this day of fighting had ended, it is said that Sherman came upon Grant sitting under a tree quietly whittling a piece of wood with a knife. Sherman reflected on the terrible battle they had just waged and remarked, "Well, Grant, we've had the devil's own day, haven't we?" Grant, unphased, shot back his quiet and completely calm response, "Yes. Lick 'em tomorrow, though."

Thousands had already died on both sides, but nevertheless, the fighting began anew the following day. With the Union Army swelled by reinforcements, they were able to push the Confederates all the way back to their base in Corinth, Mississippi. Grant and the Union had won this major engagement. But the victory itself did not really change the situation on the ground.

The Confederates were forced back to where they had already been stationed in the vicinity of Corinth, and the Union troops, for the time, remained where they had been, at Pittsburg Landing. It seemed as if many lives had been lost just for a bitter stalemate to take root. Nevertheless, Grant and company began a slow advance toward the Confederate positions in Corinth all the same.

The Battle of Shiloh saw over twenty-three thousand dead and wounded; at that point in the war, it was the bloodiest battle yet. After criticism over the high casualities at Shiloh, General Halleck wanted to be cautious. Some would say overly cautious. It has been said that during this slow crawl to Corinth, the Union Army was moving less than a mile a day. The reason for their slowness was that, every so often, Halleck had them stop and dig up trenches so that they could fall back on them if necessary.

Such a thing would have been useful if they were forced to make a hasty retreat, but at this point, the Confederates were not in any shape to launch a major offensive. Grant himself believed that the troops should just charge at Corinth all at once rather than crawling along digging trenches. He thought that the city would have easily fallen to the Union forces in just a couple of days' time. Nevertheless, they pushed on at their snail's pace.

Then, in mid-May, Grant thought he saw a means of making a breakthrough. He saw that there was a point of weakness in the Confederate lines. Grant mentioned the opening to Halleck and tried to persuade him to send his forces to charge this weakened portion of their enemy. Halleck only treated Grant's suggestion with contempt, allegedly stating that such a thing was "too stupid" to consider.

At any rate, by May 30th, Corinth was finally in sight. But by the time the Union troops had arrived, the Confederates were already making their getaway. Upon arrival, the Union soldiers were confronted not with Confederate soldiers but merely makeshift dummies the Confederates had made and put in place the day before. These dummies were like scarecrows. Old, tattered uniforms had been stuffed with hay and put on guard to face their frustrated foes. The Union had taken Corinth, but the men did not have much of a victory to show for their efforts.

However, the retreating Confederates were not far away, and Grant believed that the cavalry could easily intercept them. To his chagrin, Halleck absolutely refused to entertain this notion. The cautious Halleck must have thought that such a thing was "too stupid" to consider as well.

Ulysses S. Grant and company were now forced to sit tight on this unattractive stretch of trench-surrounded terrain. Grant was growing tired of the friction he was experiencing with General Halleck, and he actually requested to take some time off. However, he was convinced by Sherman not to do so. Sherman and Grant had become quite close during the last few months of fighting, and Sherman could not stand the thought of Grant leaving now. With some effort, Sherman was ultimately able to convince Grant to stay right where he was.

In the meantime, Grant received some major news from Washington. Halleck was being summoned to DC to take over for George McClellan. He would become the general in chief. Grant would take over as the top dog of the Union forces in the Western Theater.

In the immediate aftermath of Shiloh, Grant was widely hailed as a heroic commander. But once it sunk in with the public just how horribly high the casualty rate was, opinions began to change. Shortly thereafter, many newspaper outlets began to criticize Ulysses S. Grant for the high mortality rate, and some even accused him of being drunk at the time. Some in the press seized upon this, ridiculing General Ulysses S. Grant as a drunk who did not really know what he was doing.

Grant said very little about the criticism, but his father could not remain quiet. He was disturbed by the attacks being launched against his son, and he actually wrote to several of the major papers, demanding for them to cease their criticism. Grant did not take kindly to his father standing up for him. He had to remind his dad that he was an adult who could defend himself, and he asked him to just let the matter drop.

Embarrassed by his dad's efforts to defend him, Grant told his father, "I have not an enemy in the world who has done me so much injury in your efforts at my defense. I require no defenders and for my sake let me alone. Do nothing to correct what you have already done, but for the future keep quiet upon this subject." Grant was indeed worried about the criticism, but he continued to keep his head down. And soon, the worst of the storm had passed.

Chapter 9 – The Taking of Vicksburg

"I have never advocated war—except as a means of peace."

-Ulysses S. Grant

After the capture of Corinth and receiving his promotion, Grant took up residence in Memphis, Tennessee. Although the city was now in Union hands, its residents were most certainly not showing any "Southern hospitality" to the occupying Northerners. In fact, the local people were occasionally openly hostile. Nevertheless, Grant was able to settle in. And not only that, he was even able to have Julia and their children come to stay with him as well.

They came along right around Independence Day. Grant and company made sure that July 4th, 1862, was one to remember, with fireworks in the air and festivity on the ground. Shortly thereafter, Grant decided to move back to Corinth. There, he was able to procure one of the nicest homes in town.

He was given the house of a wealthy local by the name of Francis E. Whitfield, who had been caught sending mail to Confederate operatives. This caused him to get arrested by the Union authorities. Whitfield was then asked to take an oath of loyalty to the Union, but he refused to do so. This defiance bought him a ticket to a holding cell in Alton, Illinois. Grant moved into the detained man's home and used it as a temporary headquarters. Julia and the kids followed. They arrived by rail from Memphis shortly after Grant had procured the house.

All seemed well and good until Grant's father, Jesse, decided he had a problem with his grandkids taking up shelter in what he termed to be a rough-and-tumble army camp full of rough-and-tumble men. Grant had to write his father back to explain to him that he and his family were not actually sleeping in some tent with a bunch of drunken troops. Grant wrote the old man, "They are not running around camp among all sorts of people, but we are keeping house in the property of a truly loyal secessionist who has been furnished free board and lodging at Alton, Illinois; here the children see nothing but the greatest propriety."

Everything was relatively calm at Ulysses S. Grant's new residence, but there were some instances in which Grant witnessed bouts of chaos from his own troops. On one occasion, he was standing with his staff officers when he heard the sound of women screaming. Grant went out to investigate and saw the source of the commotion. To his horror, one of his own Union soldiers was chasing after a couple of local residents—a mother and daughter—waving his musket in the air as he pursued them.

Grant was not sure what the troublemaker was up to, but he knew it must not have been good. Grant rushed toward the soldier, grabbed the man's weapon right out of his hands, and then proceeded to beat the man over the head with his own firearm. The delinquent soldier was knocked out from the exchange, prompting an aide to remark, "I guess you have killed him, General." To which Grant gruffly replied, "If I have, it has only served him right." If Ulysses S. Grant hated anything, he hated the sight of innocent civilians being bullied by occupying troops. Any time he saw an instance of it, he was sure to respond.

However, Grant would soon have more to worry about than his own disorderly troops. He received word that Confederate General Sterling Price was bringing Confederate troops in the vicinity of the town of Iuka, Mississippi, which was some twenty miles southeast of Corinth. It seemed as if he was readying them to smash into the Union positions in northern Mississippi.

Grant was concerned about these developments, and it has been said that he spent most of the following evening pouring over all of the latest bits of information about the enemy movements on the field. Grant was certain that the Confederates were attempting to launch a major offensive in the hopes that they could deal a decisive blow against the Union Army. As the days wore on, it was then determined that Price was most likely coordinating with another Confederate commander by the name of Earl Van Dorn.

It seemed that Price might be trying to draw Union troops away from Corinth so that Van Dorn could launch a separate attack against the town. After several days of brainstorming, by September, Grant had developed his game plan. He decided that they would have to deliver a two-pronged assault that would take out the forces led by Price while simultaneously taking on the troops of Van Dorn.

Grant arranged to have one regiment led by a certain Edward Ord sent to take on the Confederates at Iuka while having another contingent under the guidance of William S. Rosecrans tackle the rest. However, once this plan was executed, there was almost immediately a problem. Heavy rains came down and slowed the march of Rosecrans's troops. Nevertheless, Grant believed that Edward Ord's troops might be able to delay Price long enough to make up for it.

In the meantime, on September 18th, Grant and his men had received news that there had been a Union victory in Sharpsburg, Maryland, against Robert E. Lee's famed Army of Northern Virginia. Grant had Ord send this news off to Price in the hopes that it might pressure the Confederate to surrender. Price refused, though, making it clear that such things made no difference to him.

At any rate, on September 19th, Rosecrans and his men reached Iuka and engaged the enemy. The Confederates proved too strong for him, and Rosecrans and company had to pull back. The Confederates then withdrew from their positions on September 20th. Although the enemy had gotten away, their advance was halted, and they were clearly defeated in battle.

Grant was also assured that Corinth had been secured. However, the fighting would erupt again just north of Corinth on October 3rd, but after two days of terrific warfare, the forces of both Van Dorn and Price were soundly defeated. Grant was disappointed, though, because a large group of Rebels was once again allowed to retreat. They fled back to their strongholds in Mississippi.

Grant would later remark in disappointment and disgust, "I cannot see how the enemy are to escape without losing everything but their small arms." But yet, once again, they did indeed slip away. Nevertheless, the war went on. On October 25th, 1862, Grant took over the command of the entire District of Tennessee. With this new command came a new headquarters, and Grant and his family ended up moving into a new home in the quaint but charming little town of La Grange that November.

Grant's next objective would be to go on the offensive and drive the Confederates out of a little-known place called Vicksburg. Vicksburg was a Confederate stronghold situated farther south on the east bank of the Mississippi River. If the Union troops could gain control of the fortress at Vicksburg, they would have control of the entire Mississippi River.

The Union troops would first converge on the nearby settlement of Holly Springs. They expected a fight, but the Confederates actually evacuated the place on November 9th. As such, when the Union troops arrived a few days later on the 13th, they found it all but deserted. Always on the move, Grant then held council with Sherman on November 21st in Columbus, Kentucky, before returning to his headquarters.

He was indeed a man on the march, going from this place to that. As he told his father in a written letter at the time, "I will again be in motion. I feel every confidence of success but I know that a heavy force is now to my front." Along with his concerns over the upcoming operation against the Confederates, Grant was also increasingly worried about the actions of the occupying Union troops under his command. After a particularly bad spate of incidences of harassment conducted by his own men, Grant was heard to remark, "Houses have been plunder'd and burned down, fencing destroyed and citizens frightened without enquiry as to their status in the Rebellion."

Having an occupying army camped out in your neighborhood is never an easy thing to deal with. It is even more difficult when the average citizen is being judged on whether or not they were loyal to the occupiers—it created an understandably toxic atmosphere. Grant was ready to rein in these trespasses, reminding his troops that any violators of the common peace would be dealt with and prosecuted accordingly. All the same, sabotage conducted by Southern sympathizers was a real threat, and Grant had to keep a constant eye out for this as well.

Grant's trusty fellow General William Tecumseh Sherman would take on the Confederates just north of Vicksburg at a place called Chickasaw Bayou on December 29th, 1862. However, the operation did not go well, and the Confederate commander, Lieutenant General John C. Pemberton, ended up pushing Sherman's group back.

However, Union General John Alexander McClernand was able to connect with Sherman's battered troops. With some effort, they managed to seize the enemy fortress—Fort Hindman—in early January of 1863. Grant appeared on the scene in Memphis on January 10th. McClernand had taken the initiative at Fort Hindman, and once Grant found out, he was infuriated. Grant wanted all the forces to focus on Vicksburg and felt that the seizure of Fort Hindman was an unnecessary distraction.

In fact, Ulysses S. Grant was so upset that he sent off a dispatch to Halleck, declaring that the rogue McClernand had "gone on a wild goose chase." Grant then sent a message to McClernand himself, ordering him, "Unless you are acting under authority not derived from me keep your command where it can soonest be assembled for the renewal of the attack on Vicksburg."

Sherman, while under the command of McClernand, carried out a successful attack on Fort Hindman a short time later, on January 12th. This victory gained a fortress as well as some five thousand Confederate prisoners of war. After this achievement, Grant received a cable from Halleck, which suggested that he should take over for General McClernand. Halleck stated, "You are hereby authorized to relieve General McClernand from command of the expedition against Vicksburg, giving it to the next in rank, or taking it yourself."

This was exactly what Grant wanted to hear. He would now lead the charge in the offensive of Vicksburg. Grant mobilized his forces and had them set up shop in a place called Milliken's Bend in Louisiana. This town was about twenty miles northwest of Vicksburg, so it made for an excellent staging area for the coming Union invasion. The biggest hardship of this spot was the fact that the site was surrounded by water.

Vicksburg itself is said to have been positioned some two hundred feet high over the Mississippi. It was nestled on a bluff that was situated on the east side of that great river. Here, it is said that the Mississippi takes a sharp turn, encompassing Vicksburg. This puts Vicksburg in a prime position for defense since artillery can be swung around at all points of approach. Having said that, it was realized that while heavily armored attack ships could sneak by, they would not be able to engage in a direct assault on the battlements.

A land invasion would be difficult as well since much of the terrain was treacherous swamplands. Grant would spend the next several weeks trying to find a way to break through to Vicksburg. He finally determined to send a daring squadron of craft shepherded by ironclad gunboats racing across the river past the Vicksburg artillery. They were supposed to land just south of Vicksburg. Since all of Vicksburg's guns were aimed at the river, once this dangerous waterway was traversed, a march through the "back door" of Vicksburg would be relatively easy by comparison.

This squadron was led by naval commander David Dixon Porter on April 16th, 1863. In the end, only one ship was lost. The boats, which were stocked full of ammunition and other supplies, safely crossed through this dangerous gauntlet with their ironclad gunboat escorts. On April 17th, Ulysses S. Grant ordered Colonel Benjamin H Grierson to launch a daring raid that would tear into Confederate positions at Jackson, Mississippi. He would then march all the way to Baton Rouge, Louisiana, thereby creating a great distraction for the Confederate forces.

In the meantime, Grant and the land invasion forces were on the move. By April 29th, they were near that so-called "backdoor" to Vicksburg with an army of forty thousand men. They were some twenty miles south of the fortress and heading north. The plan was going off without a hitch. Grant would attack Vicksburg from the south while the guns were facing in the opposite direction toward the river. The Confederate land forces were being diverted to Baton Rouge because of Colonel Grierson's simultaneously coordinated attack.

Grant launched an all-out assault on Vicksburg on May 22nd, 1863, but faced stiffer resistance than he had anticipated and temporarily had to back away. Even so, Vicksburg was surrounded by Union troops, and Grant realized it was just a matter of time before the besieged fortress would be forced to surrender. This realization was confirmed on June 28th when Grant received some inside information from a few Rebel deserters. They informed the Union troops that there was only enough food at the fort to sustain the defenders for a few more days at most.

And sure enough, on July 1st, the captain of the fort, John C. Pemberton, agreed to cease hostilities. The final terms of Vicksburg's surrender were then worked out on July 3rd, 1863. With Vicksburg's surrender complete, Grant was handed over some 32,000 prisoners of war and 172 pieces of artillery. Grant's great victory came just in time for that year's Independence Day celebration. And when Washington, DC, learned of these happenings the following day, on July 4th, it was indeed a cause for celebration.

This news, coupled with the deflection of George Pickett's charge at Gettysburg on July 3rd, made it clear to all concerned that the tide had turned. After so much bloodshed and struggle, the war was winnable. The Union was confident that it could win this war; it was now just a matter of how long it might take to do so.

Chapter 10 – The Civil War Comes to an End

"In every battle there comes a times when both sides consider themselves beaten, then he who continues the attack wins."

-Ulysses S. Grant

Ulysses S. Grant's success at Vicksburg was a stunning achievement, and unlike Shiloh, the remarks on the battle would be positive. President Lincoln and even Grant's old agitator, General Halleck, had kind words to say about Grant's leadership. Grant was given yet another promotion, becoming a major general. And if that wasn't enough, on October 16th, 1863, he was given command over the entire Division of the Mississippi. This meant that Grant had jurisdiction over the entire Western Theater of the war.

Grant was now in his early forties, and with such a high rank in the US Army, that meant he was basically set for life. The rank came with a salary of some $6,000 a year, which in those days was a lot of money, considering the fact that a regular low-ranking soldier in the Union Army, on average, made less than $600 a year.

But all accolades aside, Grant was ready to further wage war. The Union forces had been recently repelled during the Battle of Chickamauga, and after a tactical withdrawal, the Union battalion dubbed the Army of the Cumberland were forced to hole up in Chattanooga. Union Major General Joseph Hooker led a contingent of troops to relieve the besieged fighters. Once the Army of the Cumberland was freed, Grant had General Sherman lead the Army of the Tennessee and join forces with them so they could march on Confederate positions at Missionary Ridge.

Fierce fighting erupted on November 23rd, 1863, when Union troops led by Major General George Henry Thomas came upon Confederates positioned to the north of the ridge, which was some distance south of Chattanooga. The Confederates were not prepared to face the Union soldiers and immediately retreated back to Missionary Ridge. Union troops then dug into place at a spot called Orchard Knob and prepared to launch an assault on Missionary Ridge itself.

In the meantime, General Sherman was preparing his troops to cross the Tennessee River to bolster the Union assault on Missionary Ridge. The following day, on November 24th, Sherman's group stalled and was unable to advance in time. Another Union general—Joseph Hooker—managed to seize a strategic position on Lookout Mountain, which allowed the Union to jump out in front of the Confederate lines.

Grant ordered Thomas to charge the Confederate positions at Missionary Ridge on the 25th. After a complicated, coordinated effort, in which Thomas took much initiative, the Confederates were defeated. The Union troops had thereby managed to gain dominance over all of Tennessee and had a clear path to march on the Confederate stronghold of Georgia. Grant would end up spending the winter in Nashville, Tennessee, and Julia would stay with him.

During her time in Nashville, Grant's wife began to volunteer at the army hospital, tending to the many wounded soldiers. Seeing all of these wounded men really made an impression on her about the true cost of the war. But whenever she mentioned her experiences at the hospital to Grant, he did not seem to want to hear much about it. In fact, Grant is said to have told her on one occasion, "Now, my dear, I don't want to hear anything about that. I don't want you to come to me with any of these tales of the hospitals. I have all I can bear up under outside my home, and when I come to you I want to see you and the children and talk about other matters. I want to get all the sunshine I can."

Grant was a pragmatic and practical man. He understood the horrors of war, but he also understood the necessity of not dwelling on such things while one was in the midst of a terrible conflict. Like many military men, past and present, Grant had learned to compartmentalize some of the more difficult aspects of his life.

Although Nashville is a Southern city, the winter of 1863/64 proved to be a cold one. And this, along with Grant's occasionally chilly disposition, prompted Julia to leave Nashville for the "warmer" climate of St. Louis. Ulysses S. Grant was left to his own machinations in the spring of 1864, and he deeply contemplated how the war was shaping up.

Grant received word on March 2nd that President Abraham Lincoln had given him yet another promotion, this time to lieutenant general. This was a major advancement, as it essentially gave Grant the ability to direct the Union Army as a whole. Grant left for DC shortly thereafter.

There is a story that Grant arrived at the prestigious Willard Hotel on March 8th, 1864. He was accompanied by his fourteen-year-old son, Fred, and he was initially unrecognized by the clerk. Grant, who had eschewed ostentatious, decorated uniforms ever since a local troublemaker in Ohio mocked him after his graduation from West Point, did not dress to impress. In fact, his wrinkled, standard-issue uniform made him look like some dingy, run-of-the-mill soldier.

But after Grant signed his name at the front desk, the clerk began singing a different tune and attempted to offer him the best room in the house. After Grant checked in and tucked his tired child into bed, he came back down to the lobby, where he was greeted by a throng of curious well-wishers. Just like today, word in Washington travels fast.

Eventually, however, Grant was able to make his way over to the White House, where President Lincoln was waiting for him. Grant was directed to the East Room, where a reception had been arranged for him. Lincoln himself strode right up to Grant, took him by the hand, and led him over to the First Lady who was waiting nearby and remarked, "Why look, Mother—here is General Grant."

Lincoln had indeed heard much of the war hero, and he was thrilled to finally have his winning general standing before him. The pair made a striking contrast physically, with Grant being short and slightly stout while Lincoln was tall and trim. Ulysses S. Grant, whose habitual slouching made him appear even shorter than his five feet, seven inches frame otherwise would have conveyed, was so short that, at one point, Lincoln had him stand up on a couch. This was done so that others in the room could have a better look at the great victor of Vicksburg.

There was plenty of small talk, but the serious discussions came later that night when Lincoln sat down privately with Grant to have a word with him. The most important thing that the president covered was the level of autonomy and authority that he was giving Grant. Some presidents, even to this day, would prefer to be in the driver's seat as the commander in chief and dictate to their generals what to do. Others have a more hands-off style in which they delegate authority to their most trusted subordinates and allow them to make important decisions themselves.

Lincoln made it clear to Grant that he trusted him enough to think for himself. President Lincoln assured General Grant that he had full confidence in his ability to lead the troops and would leave the most immediate decisions on the field for him to decide. The next day, Grant was given his commission in a formal ceremony at which Lincoln was present.

In his acceptance speech, Ulysses S. Grant's words, like usual, were brief, modest, and to the point. To Lincoln and everyone else who had gathered to hear him speak, Grant remarked, "Mr. President: I accept this commission with gratitude for the high honor conferred. With the aid of the noble armies that have fought on so many fields for our common country, it will be my earnest endeavor not to disappoint your expectations. I feel the full weight of the responsibilities now devolving on me and know that if they are met it will be due to those armies, and above all to the favor of that Providence which leads both nations and men."

After leaving DC, Grant set up a new headquarters in nearby Culpepper, Virginia, where he would preside over General George Meade's Army of the Potomac. Due to the wide availability of the telegraph, Grant did not intend to stay in one spot for long. As

Grant wistfully remarked in a letter to his father at the time, "In these days of telegraphy and steam I can command whilst traveling and visiting about."

Yes, the ability to hop on a train to receive updates of various positions on the field from telegraph posts all along the tracks certainly changed the way in which a war could be run. But if Grant thought he would be free to move as he pleased, he would find this to be more wishful thinking than reality.

Nevertheless, Grant would orchestrate the greatest battle yet to come—an attack on Robert E. Lee's formidable Army of Northern Virginia. In early May, Grant led a contingent of troops across the Rapidan River, and they began to make their way farther south. The group then found themselves in wilderness-like conditions, as they had to march across rugged terrain.

Lee did not try to hinder the crossing of Union troops over the Rapidan. But as soon as they were on this rough, uneven ground, Lee decided to let them have it. Grant and company were immediately repulsed off the main roads and forced to take shelter in the surrounding woods. Many in the Union—and most likely the Confederate—Army thought that Grant should retreat back across the river, but he refused.

Instead, he urged his men to engage in an all-out assault the following day. Grant's group sustained heavy casualties, but Grant refused to give up. Later that evening, he and his troops moved under cover of darkness to Lee's rightmost flank and then south behind Confederate lines. Lee was initially taken aback by this outflanking maneuver, but he quickly recovered and rapidly sent his troops to confront the Union forces near the site of Spotsylvania.

Here, the fighting bitterly continued from May 8th all the way until May 20th, with both sides delivering a blistering barrage. It was brutal, but Grant refused to give up. He actually fired off a note to General Halleck on May 11th, in which he plainly stated his determination, declaring, "I propose to fight it out on this line if it takes all summer." But as the dead and wounded continued to pile up, the specter of that bloody Battle of Shiloh began to return.

It has been said that at this point, the Union may have lost as many as eighteen thousand troops, whereas the Confederates had lost around twelve thousand. Even though the losses were greater on the Union side, the Confederate losses were more painful since they had a much more limited pool of troops to rely on.

Although it was true the Union was better equipped to raise troops, that did not mean that soldiers were expendable enough to be herded through meat grinders. The word "butcher" began to be leveled at Grant by some of his own subordinates behind his back. Nevertheless, Grant was determined to continue.

Grant once again attempted an outflanking maneuver, but Lee was too quick and immediately responded to counteract it. This led to another bloody day of close, brutal combat between both sides. However, Robert E. Lee's army was quickly losing steam, and by June, he and his men were forced to make a tactical retreat to Richmond. Ulysses S. Grant and the Union Army remained in hot pursuit, with the Union forces coming as close as six miles to Richmond by June 2nd.

Lee knew that he could not sustain any more heavy losses, so he decided to hunker down in Richmond and prepare for a standoff. Lee had trenches dug and fortifications erected as he waited for a final clash with the Union. On the following day, Grant ordered a full-frontal assault on the Confederate positions. However, the Union troops were unable to break the Confederate lines, so a new strategy was needed.

Shifting gears, Grant led his army across the James River on June 14th and attempted to take the town of Petersburg, which was situated just south of Richmond. Petersburg was defended by a force of some 1,500 troops led by Confederate General P. G. T. Beauregard.

Grant's Union contingent easily outnumbered this group, but Beauregard's forces fought so ferociously that they held off long enough for Lee to rush over with what was left of the Army of Northern Virginia. Grant's weary troops were not ready for another large clash, so the two sides ended up settling into yet another protracted standoff.

In the midst of this intensity, Ulysses S. Grant had his army engineers construct what has been termed a veritable "city of wooden huts." In the center of all of this was Grant's headquarters, from which he would command his massive army. Incredibly enough, despite the nature of the war zone, Grant had considered the status quo of the stalemate stable enough and had his wife and children come join him as he oversaw the siege's progress.

The base camp that was constructed was impressive, and its very existence, along with the overwhelming advantage of Union numbers, would make a visitor to the encampment wonder why the stalemate even existed. Grant, for one, would have been quick to point out the reason—the Confederates had the edge over them due to their interior lines. This means that as long as the Confederates had control of the innermost part of their battlements, they could have reinforcements—as meager as they might have been—quickly rushed off to one side or the other in the advent of a sudden Union charge. So, even if they were outnumbered, the Union troops would face a bloody battle upon their approach.

Grant knew this well enough, and it was for this reason that he was willing to wait the Confederates out before attempting another full-frontal assault. This point was perfectly illustrated by an incident that occurred in July, in which one of the Union engineers managed to dig under the Confederate defensive positions and plant a mine. The mine blew up a short time later, killing hundreds of Confederate troops.

Right after this, the Union troops attempted to charge into the site where the bomb had gone off, but as soon as they did, the Confederates quickly reacted. They let loose with a wild barrage of gunfire, killing many of the Union troops who charged forward. The situation was so bad that some described it as being akin to "shooting fish in a barrel."

The Confederates must have known deep down that the battle was ultimately theirs to lose. They knew that even if the Union pulled back and resorted to slowly chipping away at them rather than engaging in a full-on assault, it would be just a matter of time. And General Ulysses S. Grant knew that the main objective had been accomplished; it was just a matter of fulfilling it.

In the meantime, he had all manner of visitors come to pay him his respects right there on the battlefield. Along with his wife and children, none other than President Abraham Lincoln stopped by, arriving by steamboat. One of these meetings was actually captured by a photographer, depicting Lincoln and Grant in the midst of conversation, although in the image you might not know it. In that particular frame, the two appear to be sharing a quiet, somber moment with serious expressions on their faces.

It was not until April of 1865 that the siege finally began to break. The dwindling Confederate forces realized that they could no longer sustain their positions near Richmond. When Confederate President Jefferson Davis fled from the capital of the Confederacy on April 2ⁿᵈ, General Lee and the surviving Confederate forces followed suit, heading off to Lynchburg, Virginia.

Richmond was now firmly in Union hands, and the rest of the South would soon follow. All that remained was to force General Robert E. Lee to surrender what remained of the tattered Army of Northern Virginia. Grant sought to do this without wasting any more bullets. Instead of firing off weapons, he fired off a letter to Lee, beseeching him to give up. Here is Grant's letter to Lee in full:

"The results of the last week must convince you of the hopelessness of further resistance on the part of the Army of Northern Virginia in this struggle. I feel that it is so, and regard it as my duty to shift from myself the responsibility of any further effusion of blood, by asking of you the surrender of that portion of the Confederate States army known as the Army of Northern Virginia."

Lee immediately responded back, and he was very careful with his words. He acknowledged the desperation but tried to make things better than they were by stating that he was "not entertaining the opinion you express on the hopelessness of further resistance." At the same time, though, Lee faced reality enough to agree that it was also his "desire to avoid a useless effusion of blood."

It was this understanding that would lead these two men from opposing sides of the war to meet at Virginia's now-famous Appomattox Court House on April 9ᵗʰ, 1865. Here, these two men who had served together as comrades some twenty years prior in the Mexican-American War met as the leaders of two opposing armies. The meeting of the two men is said to have been gracious enough, and after a quick expenditure of pleasantries, the two generals hammered out the terms that would finally end the American Civil War.

Grant, of course, insisted on a full and unconditional surrender, but he was forgiving enough to allow the Southern fighters a road back to normalcy. Rather than locking them all up as prisoners of war, Grant stipulated that the Confederate troops could be placed on a conditional form of parole. Grant's written directive stated that these former Confederates were "not to be disturbed by U.S. authority so long as they observe their paroles and the laws in force where they may reside."

The terms were generous enough for the battered and weary Confederate General Robert E. Lee, and he approved of them, signing his name to the agreement. Ulysses S. Grant felt so strongly about rehabilitating the Southerners who had rebelled that he even ordered his troops not to rejoice at their victory in order to avoid further animosity between them and their vanquished opponents.

The forty-two-year-old General Grant was trying hard to put the pieces of the country back together, but a terrible event would occur just days later that would make the nation once again feel as if it had been torn asunder. On April 14th, 1865, President Abraham Lincoln would be shot. He would die the very next morning.

Chapter 11 – Grant's Role as Lincoln's Successor

"I suffer the mortification of seeing myself attacked right and left by people at home professing patriotism and love of country who have never heard the whistle of a hostile bullet. I pity them and the nation dependent on such for its existence. I am thankful, however that, though such people make a great noise, the masses are not like them."

-Ulysses S. Grant

Ulysses S. Grant, like much of the rest of the country, was absolutely shocked by what had happened to Abraham Lincoln. But even more shocking for Grant was the circumstances surrounding the event. As all of the history books tell us, President Lincoln was shot at Ford's Theatre during an evening in which he, his wife, and other close associates were enjoying some much-needed rest.

Everyone was intently watching the play unfold on stage when Confederate zealot and well-known actor John Wilkes Booth took the spotlight from the stage. He entered Lincoln's box, shot the president in the head, and jumped on the stage, shouting, "Sic semper tyrannis!"

Prior to attending this event, Lincoln had held a cabinet meeting that very day in which Grant was in attendance. After the cabinet meeting dispersed, Lincoln took Grant aside and invited him and his wife to attend that very production at Ford Theatre later that night. Grant was not sure if he could make it, but he conferred with his wife. Julia said she had other plans and told her husband that she was taking their son Jesse with her to Burlington that evening.

This gave Grant the perfect excuse not to attend, and Lincoln, with his natural patience and understanding nature, told Grant that was perfectly fine. One must wonder, of course, what might have transpired if Grant was seated beside Lincoln when the assassin's bullet struck. Ulysses S. Grant himself certainly must have wondered.

At any rate, Ulysses and Julia had just gotten off at a train station in Philadelphia when a telegram was rushed over to Grant informing him of what happened. It has been said that the blood appeared to drain from Ulysses S. Grant's face as he realized that the president had been shot. Lincoln was not yet dead at this point, but it was clear to all involved that it was a mortal injury.

Grant, like many, shared a dark and desperate sentiment. The nation had finally been led through the terrible civil war only to see the man who led them through it perish. Abraham Lincoln, who had been reelected in 1864, was the one everyone thought would rebuild the nation after the war ended, yet that hope was dashed.

After his passing, President Lincoln's funeral was held on April 19th, 1865, and General Ulysses S. Grant was there, overseeing the ceremony. Grant was largely known for being stoic and unemotional, but on this sad day, he did not hold back and was seen openly crying.

With Lincoln's death, his vice president, Andrew Johnson, took over, which was a prospect that Grant was not too thrilled about. Grant knew that the true way to rebuild the country was to follow Lincoln's approach of leniency toward the Southerners. He knew that a harsh peace would only prolong hostilities and internal discord. Grant feared that Johnson might upend his and Lincoln's efforts of reconciliation by exacting draconian measures against the Southerners.

However, shortly into President Johnson's administration, Grant began to warm up to the presidential newcomer. At one point, he is said to have remarked, "I have every reason to hope that in our new

President we will find a man disposed and capable of conducting the government in its old channel."

Grant wanted the continuity of Lincoln's agenda more than anything, but Johnson would ultimately disappoint him on this front. The two men would come to blows over Johnson's harshness on June 7th, 1865, when Grant famously defended his former adversary Robert E. Lee. President Johnson had Lee indicted by a grand jury for his rebellion and was ready to have Lee executed on charges of the "high crime of treason against the United States."

In Johnson's hard line against the Rebels, he wanted to make Lee an example to others. Grant was horrified at these developments and immediately made his way to the White House to tell President Johnson that Lee's life should be secure under the agreement that he had made with Lee at that Appomattox Court House at the end of the war.

In fact, Grant was so enraged that he told President Johnson he would quit rather than see Lee prosecuted. This finally prompted Johnson to reconsider, and the charges against Robert E. Lee were ultimately dropped. It was not the first time that the two men would clash. Another terrible exchange emerged in August of 1867 after Johnson fired the secretary of war, Edwin Stanton, and made Grant the interim secretary.

Grant did not approve of Stanton's dismissal, but he felt it was his duty to comply, so he filled the new role. This was not the end of the story, though. President Johnson's overreach had never been approved by the Senate. This resulted in Congress voting to bring Stanton back in December of 1867. Edwin Stanton was then officially placed back in his position on January 10th, 1868.

Grant realized the bind he was in, and he informed Johnson that he needed to quit the role of secretary of war in order to follow procedure. Johnson disagreed and argued that he would be able to overturn the results. He urged Grant to stay on board. Nevertheless, a short time later, Grant made good on his threat to quit and resigned. Johnson was infuriated with Grant, feeling that he had betrayed him. During an emotionally charged cabinet meeting, he actually went on to denounce Grant as untrustworthy, speaking at length of his supposed duplicity.

All of these shenanigans would lead to President Andrew Johnson's own impeachment. Johnson would end up beating impeachment but just barely—he avoided it by just a single vote. Despite all of the chaos, Grant was not viewed as a bad character in all this. Grant was viewed as an honorable stalwart of the rule of law, which means he was far from being seen as being duplicitous.

Grant had long been considered a potential contender for the presidency, and the grace and character that he had presented through this political storm only helped his star to rise. This was why in the election of 1868, Grant became a shoo-in for becoming the next Republican candidate for president. And sure enough, at the 1868 Republican National Convention held in Chicago that year, Grant was nominated to be at the top of the ticket for the party.

Ulysses S. Grant was a reluctant candidate, but he also felt a strong conviction that this could be his opportunity to make sure that Abraham Lincoln's legacy was followed. Grant ultimately won the election, receiving 214 electoral college votes compared to his opponent—Horatio Seymour's—80 votes. He was sworn into office on March 4th, 1869. The forty-six-year-old Ulysses S. Grant was now ready for a new title—President of the United States.

Upon becoming president, one of the first major pieces of legislation that Grant championed was the Fifteenth Amendment. This amendment to the US Constitution sought to give every male citizen "regardless of race, color, or previous condition of servitude" the right to vote. It is worth noting that this amendment did not give *women* the right to vote—only males. Women would not be given the right to vote until 1920.

Another achievement of Grant's presidency was the Ku Klux Klan Act of 1871, which sought to shut down the Southern-spawned terrorist organization that had been intimidating and terrorizing the post-Civil War South. Prior to this act, such crimes were handled at the local level, with very few meaningful results. This bit of legislation allowed the federal government as a whole to go after dangerous domestic groups such as the Ku Klux Klan (KKK).

This was especially important as it pertained to the Ku Klux Klan since the KKK was established in the South as a violent group hellbent on repressing recently freed slaves, as well as other minorities. Grant knew all too well that the crimes of the KKK would never be rightfully prosecuted by the Southern legislatures. Grant knew that it would take a federal law to prosecute and bring the Klan members to justice. And his 1871 act was efficient in doing so.

A much less successful measure taken by Grant was his attempt to annex San Domingo or, as it is known today, the Dominican Republic. Grant argued hard for the annexation and tried to push for it in both 1870 and 1871, but the measure fell through both times. Part of Grant's reasoning for making San Domingo a state was to provide a potential safe haven for some of the recently freed African Americans of the South.

Grant also had his fair share of controversy, starting with the Crédit Mobilier scandal, which erupted in the middle of his administration in the fall of 1872. This scandal saw members of Congress engaging in insider trading. An official congressional investigation was launched, and two members of Congress were censured. President Grant himself was not directly implicated, but the scandal damaged his reputation. Nevertheless, Grant would be reelected that same year, even though the scandal would continue to swirl around his second term in office.

In 1873, shortly after he was sworn in for his next four years, the nation faced a severe economic depression. And the way that this depression was brought on was in itself a scandal. It was centered around the New York-based brokerage firm Jay Cooke and Company. Jay Cooke was an up-and-coming businessman and banker who had taken the initiative during the Civil War to buy war bonds. These operations quickly increased Cooke's prestige, and by the end of the war, he could proudly say that he had been an integral part of financing the Union effort.

After the war had ended, Cooke began to become involved with the financial operations of another juggernaut—the Northern Pacific Railway. This massive railway would span some two thousand miles from the country's midsection all the way to the western coast on the Pacific.

Needless to say, such an operation requires a lot of money, and it needed government grants in order to be completed—including land grants. Cooke ended up greasing the palms of several politicians in order to get the necessary legislation passed that enabled the allocation of millions of acres to be set aside for rail lines for the Northern Pacific. Cooke also shelled out a lot of money to the Republican National Committee to make sure that Grant was reelected in 1872.

Cooke also ran his own bank, of which Grant himself had been a customer. Ulysses S. Grant knew Cooke on a personal level, and he had even visited him at his home in Philadelphia. Grant was actually staying over at Cooke's house in September of 1873 when he received word that the Northern Pacific Railway's stocks had crashed. Cooke's own bank was the number one shareholder, so this obviously presented a big problem for him.

Nevertheless, Cooke put on a brave face before Grant and acted as if everything would be fine. However, by the time Grant got back to the White House, he was made aware of just how devastating the failure of the Northern Pacific would be. Grant was not the most astute economist, but he knew enough to realize that with such a major institution going under, a financial panic might be on the horizon.

And soon, he had to turn his attention to his secretary of the treasury—W. D. Richardson—who was attempting to prevent an all-out economic collapse. Widespread paper currency or, as it was commonly known back then, "greenbacks" were still a fairly new innovation in the United States. And as such, the idea of just printing out money was new as well.

As any economist will tell you, paper money is merely a representation of value—the more you print, the less value those greenbacks represent. And the more dollars you put in circulation, the less those dollars are worth. In turn, you will find inflated prices on everything from bread to fuel. As such, it is the role of the US Treasury to try to balance these things out.

Just prior to the Northern Pacific debacle, Secretary of the Treasury Richardson had just taken some $44 million out of circulation, reducing the number of bills available to the public to just $356 million. As treasurer, it was fully within his right to remove excess paper money. But for him to introduce more money, he would need to okay it with Congress. However, Richardson was facing a crisis, so he thought he did not have to wait for a green light from Congress. Instead, he immediately put $26 million back into circulation in an attempt to offset the collapse of the Northern Pacific Railway.

These efforts fell flat, and banks and corporations were soon going under one after the other. In some ways, this disaster had a strange unifying effect in the way that only a national crisis can. As divided as the North and South may have been from the Civil War, the whole country now shared this same burden.

But at the same time, this dire shift of the economy proved somewhat disastrous to the ongoing efforts of Reconstruction in the South. The priorities of Washington could not help but shift to the economy in general rather than rebuilding Southern institutions.

It is always a strange conundrum to fight inflation with inflation, but farmers were complaining about an inability to pay the railroad to transport their agricultural products. Congress attempted to intervene by introducing the infamous Inflation Bill. This bill would retroactively make Richardson's unilateral act of adding $26 million a part of proper protocol, and it would also add another $18 million, which bumped the total amount of bills in circulation up to $400 million.

Grant initially thought that the bill was necessary and could do some good. However, the more he contemplated the long-term effects of pumping more money into the system, the more he did not like it. And by the time the bill came to Grant's desk in the spring of 1874, he decided to veto it. Grant wrote out his thoughts at the time, stating, "It is a fair inference that if in practice this measure should fail to create the abundance of circulation expected of it, the friends of the measure, particularly those out of Congress, would clamor for [more] inflation."

In other words, Grant feared that succumbing to a supposed short-term fix of flooding the economy with more dollars would only lead to more inflation when that short-term fix proved to not be enough later on. So, with these things rattling around in his mind, Grant made up his mind to veto the bill on April 21ˢᵗ, 1874.

All of this political turmoil seemed to have helped Grant and his fellow Republicans lose the house in the 1874 midterm elections. Grant's own personal reputation had begun to slide as well. He was still admired as a war hero, but accusations of incompetence and even drunkenness were frequent lines of attack by his opponents.

The Democrats, who had been losing national elections since the Civil War, finally managed to win a majority in the House of Representatives. Since the Democratic Party was largely sympathetic to the former Confederacy, Democrat representatives began to push back against efforts to reform Southern institutions. Nevertheless, Grant managed to pass the robust Civil Rights Act of 1875, which sought to address some of the abuses being committed on the local level in the South. This would be the last bit of civil rights legislation passed until the Civil Rights Act of 1957 was signed by Republican President Dwight D. Eisenhower.

Unfortunately, by the time Grant's tenure in the White House came to an end in 1877, his efforts with civil rights legislation were being largely repressed by Southern legislatures and, on some notable occasions, even the Supreme Court. And by the time Grant's successor—Rutherford B. Hayes—became the next president, all efforts of Reconstruction were largely considered to be over.

At this point, Grant was not considering a third term, although he would eventually be pressured to give it some serious thought in the election of 1880. Upon his exit from the White House in 1877, he would leave the position of president to others. Having said that, Grant must not have been too pleased with how his successor, President Hayes, handled that last, sad chapter of Reconstruction.

Rutherford B. Hayes would remove the last federal troops from the South. These troops had been kept in place to safeguard the rights of African Americans and curb the abuses of Southern officials. But to please the Southerners, they were removed. In many ways, Hayes, although a Republican, became a conciliatory president and sought to appease the Democrats. The election of 1876 itself was shrouded in controversy due to widespread voting irregularities in Democrat-run states in the South.

Funnily enough, Grant's last act before leaving office involved fashioning an electoral commission to get to the bottom of allegations of fraud and irregularity in the 1876 election. After the commission determined that Hayes would be president, the Democrats began to cry foul.

To appease the Democratic Party, the Republicans established the so-called "Compromise of 1877," which had the last federal troops leaving the Democrat-run Southern states. As for Ulysses S. Grant? He was understandably worn down by all of the drama of the White House. Upon his exit in 1877, he was more than ready to start a brand-new chapter in his life.

Conclusion: The Pursuit of Perfection

If one were to sum up Grant's military and political career in the simplest of terms, it could be said that he was an eager and ready general but a very reluctant president. Shortly after he left office, he confided in a friend of his—John Russell Young—just what he thought about his post-political career. In reflection of his exit from DC, Grant declared, "I was never as happy in my life as the day I left the White House. I felt like a boy getting out of school."

After leaving the White House, Grant essentially took a long overdue vacation. He always wanted to travel overseas but had never had the chance to do so. Now was his time. He and his wife got on a boat, crossed the Atlantic, and embarked upon what would essentially become a world tour. He financed the trip with proceeds from a Nevada mining outfit that he had invested in. Grant had netted some $25,000 from the venture and spent just about all of it while he was abroad. This amounted to a small fortune in those days, yet Grant did not blink an eye.

However, Grant's trip was not just a vacation; it was a kind of an unofficial diplomatic mission that had him breaking bread with several important and powerful leaders of the day. He met with Queen Victoria in Britain, Pope Leo XIII in Italy, Otto von Bismarck in Germany, and even Japanese Emperor Meiji in far-off Japan. During the course of his adventure, Grant made his way over to Jerusalem, becoming the first American president to visit this great focal point of the world's three major monotheistic faiths.

Even in his youth, Ulysses S. Grant always wanted to see the world. And in his old age, he did just that. The tour came to an end when Grant and company hopped on a freighter parked off the Japanese coast and made their way across the Pacific Ocean. They ended up in Ulysses S. Grant's old stomping grounds of San Francisco on September 20th, 1879.

After this long overdue "rest," which had Grant practically circumnavigating the globe, politics once again came into the picture. Republican President Rutherford B. Hayes had pledged to serve only one term, so Grant was once again propped up as a potential candidate in the 1880 election.

At this point in American history, there was no such thing as a term limit, but it was an unspoken tradition. George Washington, the first US president, thought that a president should quit after two terms. Grant quietly insisted that he would prefer not to run, but he allowed the drama to play out. In the end, his party chose a man named James A. Garfield to be their standard-bearer instead.

This no doubt served as a great relief for Grant, who was then allowed to retire from the political scene entirely. Grant spent much of the rest of his life writing his own memoirs. Sadly, he also spent his last few years seeking to prop up a series of failed business ventures. This included—perhaps ironically, considering the debacle of the Northern Pacific during his presidency—a scheme to build a railroad in Mexico.

Grant attempted to partner with the Mexican Southern Railroad to build a new rail line from the Mexican cities of Oaxaca to Mexico City. Despite his best efforts, however, the company would ultimately go bankrupt. Grant's health began to decline shortly thereafter. He quietly passed away from a prolonged battle with cancer of the esophagus on July 23rd, 1885.

He was only sixty-three years old, and he doubtless would have lived a lot longer if it was not for his lifelong adoration of cigars. Grant had picked up the habit during his military days, and despite doctor's orders, it had stuck with him for most of his life. But despite any of his foibles and bad habits—maybe even because of them—Grant was a beloved American figure.

Grant was not perfect, but he was a man who honestly tried to do his best. And upon his death, he was remembered for these great, universally appreciated virtues. And since Grant was not perfect, he realized that America was not perfect either. But nevertheless, he believed in ceaselessly striving for a "more perfect union." Ulysses S. Grant knew that perfection was merely a work in progress, and he spent his life pursuing it. In the end, he gave his country the best he could offer, and the nation could not have asked for much more.

Here's another book by Captivating History that you might like

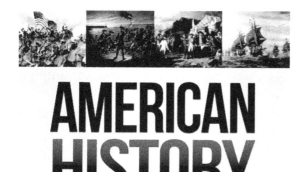

AMERICAN HISTORY

A CAPTIVATING GUIDE TO THE HISTORY OF THE
UNITED STATES OF AMERICA, AMERICAN REVOLUTION,
CIVIL WAR, CHICAGO, ROARING TWENTIES, GREAT DEPRESSION,
PEARL HARBOR, AND GULF WAR

CAPTIVATING HISTORY

Free Bonus from Captivating History
(Available for a Limited time)

Hi History Lovers!

Now you have a chance to join our exclusive history list so you can get your first history ebook for free as well as discounts and a potential to get more history books for free! Simply visit the link below to join.

Captivatinghistory.com/ebook

Also, make sure to follow us on Facebook, Twitter and Youtube by searching for Captivating History.

Resources

"Benjamin Harrison." *The White House,* https://www.whitehouse.gov/about-the-white-house/presidents/benjamin-harrison/. Accessed 9 October 2022.

"Biography of Neil Armstrong." *NASA,* 18 December 2012, https://www.nasa.gov/centers/glenn/about/bios/neilabio.html. Accessed 13 October 2022.

Boldman, Bob. "Portsmouth -Shoe Capital an Era of Growth." *Portsmouth Daily Times,* 18 January 2019, https://www.portsmouth-dailytimes.com/opinion/columns/34440/portsmouth-shoe-capital-an-era-of-growth. Accessed 6 October 2022.

Borneman, Walter R. *1812: The War That Forged a Nation.* HarperCollins, 2005.

Brace, Charles Loring. "OHJ Archive." *OHJ Archive,* https://resources.ohiohistory.org/ohj/search/display.php?page=6&ipp=20&searchterm=Array&vol=111&pages=145. Accessed 10 October 2022.

"Camp Sherman, Ohio's WWI Soldier Factory (U.S." *National Park Service,* 18 April 2020, https://www.nps.gov/articles/camp-sherman-ohio.htm. Accessed 11 October 2022.

Carter, Darnell E. "The 1904, 1906, and 1921 Race Riots in Springfield Ohio and the Hoodlum Theory." *OhioLink.edu,* 1996, https://etd.ohiolink.edu/apexprod/rws_etd/send_file/send?accession=osu1375275114&disposition=inline. Accessed 11 10 2022.

Chang, Stephen. "44nd Anniversary of the Blizzard of 1978." *National Weather Service,* https://www.weather.gov/cle/event_78blizzard. Accessed 14 October 2022.

"Cincinnati Reds History." *Baseball Almanac*, https://www.baseball-almanac.com/teams/reds.shtml. Accessed 6 October 2022.

"Civil Rights Movement." *Ohio History Central*, https://ohiohistorycentral.org/w/Civil_Rights_Movement. Accessed 13 October 2022.

"CLEVELAND: AN HISTORICAL OVERVIEW | Encyclopedia of Cleveland History." *Case Western Reserve University*, https://case.edu/ech/cleveland-historical-overview. Accessed 10 October 2022.

Cohen, Lynn. "Judith Resnik." *Jewish Women's Archive*, https://jwa.org/encyclopedia/article/resnik-judith. Accessed 14 October 2022.

"Columbus NAACP History." *NAACP Columbus, Ohio*, http://www.naacpcolumbus.org/columbus-naacp-history.html. Accessed 11 October 2022.

"Company History." *Goodyear Corporate*, https://corporate.goodyear.com/us/en/about/history.html. Accessed 7 October 2022.

Curtin, Michael F., and Joe Hallett. *The Ohio Politics Almanac*. Kent State University Press, 2015.

Czerwinski, Allegra. "6 things you didn't know about NCR's John Patterson." *Dayton.com*, 15 July 2015, https://www.dayton.com/lifestyles/things-you-didn-know-about-ncr-john-patterson/K65i9ONHk46rKchxEUN2BN/. Accessed 10 October 2022.

Dean, John W. *Warren G. Harding: The American Presidents Series: The 29th President, 1921-1923*. Edited by Arthur M. Schlesinger, Henry Holt and Company, 2004.

Derbes, Brett J. "John Hunt Morgan." *Encyclopedia of Alabama*, 16 October 2013, http://eoa.auburn.edu/article/h-3531. Accessed 4 October 2022.

"Herbert H. Dow | History." *Dow Corporate*, https://corporate.dow.com/en-us/about/company/history/herbert-henry-dow.html. Accessed 10 October 2022.

"History and Tradition." *Ohio University*, https://www.ohio.edu/admissions/about-ohio/history-traditions. Accessed 24 September 2022.

"History Lesson: Looking Back 25 Years to AmeriFlora '92." *Columbus Underground*, https://columbusunderground.com/history-lesson-looking-back-25-years-to-ameriflora-92-dm1/. Accessed 16 October 2022.

"History of the Ohio & Erie Canal (U.S." *National Park Service*, 22 November 2021, https://www.nps.gov/articles/000/history-of-the-ohio-erie-canal.htm. Accessed 28 September 2022.

"The Hocking sentinel. [volume] (Logan, Ohio) 1871-1906, April 03, 1884, Image 2." *Chronicling America*, https://chroniclingamerica.loc.gov/lccn/sn85038119/1884-04-03/ed-1/seq-2/. Accessed 9 October 2022.

"HTayor." *Harriet Taylor Upton House*, http://www.uptonhouse.org/HTayor.html. Accessed 11 October 2022.

Hurt, R. Douglas. *The Ohio Frontier: Crucible of the Old Northwest, 1720-1830*. Indiana University Press, 1998.

"Israel Ludlow." *Ohio History Central*, https://ohiohistorycentral.org/w/Israel_Ludlow. Accessed 23 September 2022.

Jakle, John A. "Cincinnati in the 1830's." *Environmental Review*, vol. 3, no. 3, 1979, pp. 2-10. *JSTOR*, https://www.journals.uchicago.edu/doi/10.2307/3984039. Accessed 28 09 2022.

Levine, Michael L. *African Americans and Civil Rights: From 1619 to the Present*. Oryx Press, 1996.

"Life – Harriet Beecher Stowe Center." *Harriet Beecher Stowe Center*, https://www.harrietbeecherstowecenter.org/harriet-beecher-stowe/harriet-beecher-stowe-life/. Accessed 1 October 2022.

"The May 4 Shootings at Kent State University: The Search for Historical Accuracy." *Kent State University*, https://www.kent.edu/may4kentstate50/may-4-shootings-kent-state-university-search-historical-accuracy. Accessed 14 October 2022.

McCullough, David. *The Pioneers: The Heroic Story of the Settlers Who Brought the American Ideal West*. Simon & Schuster, 2019.

"Moses Cleaveland." *Cleveland Historical*, https://clevelandhistorical.org/items/show/280. Accessed 21 September 2022.

"Northwest Ordinance: Primary Documents of American History (Virtual Programs & Services." *Library of Congress*, https://www.loc.gov/rr/program//bib/ourdocs/northwest.html. Accessed 18 September 2022.

O'Donnell, Patrick. "Twenty years ago today: Gunman opens fire at Wickliffe Middle school, killing one and wounding four." *Cleveland.com*, 7 November 2014, https://www.cleveland.com/metro/2014/11/twenty_years_ago_today_gunm

an.html. Accessed 16 October 2022.

"Ohio Statehood." *Ohio History Central*, https://ohiohistorycentral.org/w/Ohio_Statehood. Accessed 24 September 2022.

"Ohio Un-American Activities Committee." *Ohio History Central*, https://ohiohistorycentral.org/w/Ohio_Un-American_Activities_Committee. Accessed 12 October 2022.

"Our History." *Ohio State Fair*, https://www.ohiostatefair.com/p/about-us/our-history. Accessed 30 September 2022.

"Panic of 1819." *Ohio History Central*, http://ohiohistorycentral.org/w/Panic_of_1819. Accessed 27 September 2022.

Preston, E. D. "The Underground Railroad in Northwest Ohio." *The Journal of Negro History*, vol. 17, no. 4, 1932, pp. 409-436. *JSTOR*, https://doi.org/10.2307/2714557. Accessed 3 10 2022.

"Procter & Gamble." *Ohio History Central*, https://ohiohistorycentral.org/w/Procter_%26_Gamble. Accessed 10 October 2022.

"Profile of John Glenn." *NASA*, 3 August 2017, https://www.nasa.gov/content/profile-of-john-glenn. Accessed 13 October 2022.

"Railroads." *Ohio History Central*, https://ohiohistorycentral.org/w/Railroads. Accessed 30 September 2022.

"Rockefeller, John D. | Encyclopedia of Cleveland History." *Case Western Reserve University*, https://case.edu/ech/articles/r/rockefeller-john-d. Accessed 7 October 2022.

"Stalwarts, Half Breeds, and Political Assassination (U.S." *National Park Service*, 24 January 2021, https://www.nps.gov/articles/000/stalwarts-half-breeds-and-political-assassination.htm. Accessed 6 October 2022.

"Stokes, Carl B. | Encyclopedia of Cleveland History." *Case Western Reserve University*, https://case.edu/ech/articles/s/stokes-carl-b. Accessed 14 October 2022.

"200th Anniversary of Ohio Statehood | National Archives." *National Archives /*, https://www.archives.gov/legislative/features/ohio-statehood. Accessed 23 September 2022.

Young, Andrew. *Unwanted: A Murder Mystery of the Gilded Age*. Westholme Publishing, 2016.

Ulysses S. Grant: Triumph over Adversity, 1822-1865. Brooks D. Simpson. 2000.

Ulysses S. Grant: The Unlikely Hero. Michael Korda. 2004.

Ulysses S. Grant: Soldier and President. Geoffrey Perret. 1997.

Personal Memoirs of U. S. Grant. Ulysses S. Grant. 1885.

Grant. Ron Chernow. 2017.

To Rescue the Republic: Ulysses S. Grant, the Fragile Union, and the Crisis of 1876. Bret Baier & Catherine Whitney. 2021.

Made in United States
North Haven, CT
10 March 2023

33870841R00104